Third Edition

Getting Started in
Journalism

Jack Harkrider

L. C. Anderson High School
Austin, Texas

National Textbook Company
a division of *NTC Publishing Group* • Lincolnwood, Illinois USA

Dedication

Dr. Max R. Haddick, former journalism director of the (Texas) University Interscholastic League; Gloria Shields, long-time publications adviser at Red Oak (Texas) and North Garland (Texas) High Schools; Jim Davidson, long-standing adviser at Texas Tech University, Amarillo High School (Texas) and Lake Highlands High School (Texas); and Col. C. E. "Chuck" Savedge, "Mr. Yearbook," former adviser at Augusta Military Academy (Ft. Defiance, Virginia) were instrumental in encouraging me to enter and remain in the journalism teaching profession. It is for their constant support and to their dedication, example, and to their memory, that I dedicate this book.

Cover Photos:

top left: Jeremiah Wyka
middle left: Jeff Ellis
bottom left: Bradley Wilson
right: Jeremiah Wyka

Library of Congress Cataloging-in-Publication Data

Harkrider, Jack.
    Getting started in journalism / Jack Harkrider. — 3rd ed.
        p.   cm.
    Includes index.
    ISBN 0–8442–5952–7 (pbk.)
        1. journalism — Vocational guidance. I. Title.
PN4797.H35   1997
070.4'023 — dc20   96–23435
                                                         CIP
                                                         AC

Published by National Textbook Company, a division of NTC Publishing Group.
© 1997 NTC Publishing Group, 4255 West Touhy Avenue
Lincolnwood (Chicago), Illinois 60646-1975 U.S.A.

6 7 8 9 ML 0 9 8 7 6 5 4 3 2 1

Contents

Glossary 115

Appendix 119

Index 139

Acknowledgments

Thanks are due the following for their help and cooperation:

Judy Babb, adviser at Highland Park High School (Dallas, Texas), for her examples of feature leads and closings;

Candis Brinegar, adviser at W.B. Ray High School (Corpus Christi, Texas), and the staff of *El Tejano;*

Robert Button, former adviser at Grosse Pointe South High School (Michigan), for use of his sample staff organizational structure, and to the staff of *The Tower* for use of its outstanding publications as examples;

John Cutsinger, former adviser at Westlake High School (Austin, Texas), for his inspiration and never-ending supply of ideas and teaching techniques, and to the staff of the *Featherduster;*

Jim Davidson, former adviser at Lake Highlands High School (Richardson, Texas), for the sample job descriptions from the staff manual of *The Fang;*

Janet Elbom, adviser at A.S. Johnston High School (Austin, Texas), and the staff of *The Shiloh;*

Mark Goodman, executive director of the Student Press Law Center, for his information and analysis of the *Hazelwood v. Kuhlmeier* case;

Homer Hall, adviser at Kirkwood High School (Missouri), and the staff of *The Call;*

Nancy Hall, adviser at Shawnee Mission North High School (Kansas), for use of the journalism department's editorial policy;

Bobby Hawthorne, academic and journalism director of the University Interscholastic League, for use of the League's informational sheets, which served as guidelines for the news, feature, editorial, and headline-writing assignments;

Jim Herrington, legal counsel for the Texas chapter of the American Civil Liberties Union, for his help in explaining the concepts of student press freedom;

Susan Turner Jones, adviser at Brentwood School (Los Angeles, California), and the staff of *The Flyer;*

Lori Marks, adviser at Deerfield High School (Illinois), and the staff of *Deerprints;*

John McCartney, former adviser at Bowie High School (Austin, Texas), and the staff of the *Lone Star Dispatch;*

Dixie McGrath, former adviser at Del Valle High School (Texas), for reading and editing the manuscript and for guidance in developing the teacher's manual that accompanies this book;

Theresa Proctor, adviser at McCallum High School (Austin, Texas), for developing the six-week, nine-week, and semester lesson plans and for guidance in developing the teacher's manual that accompanies this book;

Peggy Schneider, adviser at Taylor High School (Katy, Texas), for the 20-day production plan;

The Society of Professional Journalists (SPJ) for the use of its Code of Ethics;

Paul Spadoni, adviser at Peninsula High School (Gig Harbor, Washington), and the staff of *The Outlook;*

The staff of *The Edition,* L.C. Anderson High School (Austin, Texas);

Bradley Wilson, former adviser at Wimberley (Texas) and Irving (Texas) High Schools, for his expertise and assistance in desktop publishing techniques.

I would like to extend my thanks to some other special people: Dr. William Downs, Journalism Department Chairman at Ouachita Baptist University (Arkadelphia, Arkansas), "The Wind Beneath My Wings"; Dr. Alfred Borrello, New York City author and teacher, forever a friend; Fern Maxwell, former adviser at Auburn High School (Auburn, Washington), my unofficial promotional director.

And to my wife, Gayle, for her continued support of my endeavors and to the many special journalism students, advisers, and workshop directors who have taught me so much.

1 Why Journalism?

"Stop the presses!"

Fifty years ago, that command, shouted in the city room of a large daily newspaper, meant that a reporter had a hot story—a story so big that all other work had to stop to get the story ready for the front page of the current edition. That rarely happens today. Fast-breaking events are covered by television. Newspapers follow up with the details and in-depth coverage. Still, there are big stories to cover, and the excitement of being a journalist is as real today as it has ever been.

Many of the best-known and most-respected journalists today got their start in high school, reporting for the student newspaper or the yearbook staff. Most would agree that what they learned in school proved invaluable to them in their careers.

But people who become professional journalists aren't the only ones to benefit from working on student publications or from taking part in a journalism program. Statistics show that students involved in a high school publications program, on the average, score higher in college testing programs, make better grades in college, and stay in college longer than students with no journalism background.

One of the reasons for this is that they have applied what they've learned in journalism classes in exciting and practical ways. Scholastic journalists learn to research, report, write, edit, and rewrite stories. They also learn clear and critical thinking methods, computer literacy, teamwork, research skills, and business and management techniques.

Scholastic journalism is important because it teaches practical life skills and emphasizes the absolute necessity of being informed. In addition to teaching writing and thinking methods, scholastic journalism promotes essential communication skills. When not producing future journalists, scholastic journalism produces knowledgeable consumers of the news media—consumers who will be watching, listening, and reading newspapers; who will be buying advertising, products, and ideas; who will be the leaders of the future.

Origins of Scholastic Journalism

Little did Samuel Mickle Fox realize what he started over 200 years ago. On a 4" × 6" sheet of paper, Fox penned the first issue of *The Students Gazette* on June 11, 1777, at the William Penn Charter School in Philadelphia, Pennsylvania. Published continuously until August 1778, when British soldiers closed the school, *The Gazette* is generally recognized as the first student publication in the English-speaking world.

Few, if any, school publications are handwritten today. Many school newspapers use the standard broadsheet format of the daily newspaper, about 15" wide × 24" long. Others use the mini-tab format, about 9" wide × 12" long. Most school newspapers, however, employ a 12" wide × 15" long tabloid format. Regardless of page size, most newspapers, both commercial and scholastic, adhere to a rough proportion of at least one-third longer than they are wide.

Student newspapers are printed in a variety of ways—from simple ditto and mimeograph process to sophisticated offset reproduction. Yearbooks, on the other hand, are almost always professionally printed and follow one of three formats. These formats are given in the following chart. In addition, margins are also indicated:

Size	Top Margin	Left Margin	Right Margin	Bottom Margin
9" × 12"	1"	¾"	¾"	1"
8½" × 11"	¾"	⅝"	⅝"	¾"
7¾" × 10½"	⅝"	½"	½"	⅝"

The Purpose of Scholastic Journalism

In general, a yearbook should contain pictures, and a newspaper should contain news. But there's much more to student publications than this. First, consider the purpose of a yearbook and that of a newspaper. Both publications are the laboratory products of journalism education, much as the results of a lab experiment indicate what you've learned in a chemistry class. It's possible to learn journalistic writing without producing a yearbook or a newspaper, but the laboratory experience represents the practical application of what you have learned in class. And whereas you can quickly tell whether a chemistry experiment is successful, the success or failure of a journalism experiment is best told by evaluating public reaction to the product.

Although they differ in appearance and format, yearbooks and newspapers are similar in many respects; both are journalistic products; both report on the school scene; both reflect student thought, opinion, and taste; and both give students an opportunity to bring some of their finest creative work before the public. Simply stated, the purpose of yearbooks and newspapers is to inform, enlighten, and entertain their audiences.

The fundamental difference between yearbooks and newspapers is that yearbooks serve as memory books of a certain year at a specific school and consist primarily of photographs. They are considered keepsakes. Newspapers are more current-events oriented. Unlike yearbooks, newspapers are issued several times a year, use far fewer photographs, and devote much of their content to coverage of recent events and to reporting upcoming activities. Very few students hold on to their high school newspapers for very long. The main focus of this book will center on journalistic writing and production as it applies to student newspapers.

Quill & Scroll, an international scholastic journalism society, published a study, "The Human Equation and the School Newspaper," in which the role of the school newspaper was defined as threefold:

1. To give a full account of current ideas, events, and problems affecting local secondary education.

2. To present a truthful, comprehensive, and intelligent account of the school's events in a context that gives them meaning.

3. To project a representative picture of the groups that make up the school.

Furthermore, the school newspaper serves as a forum for students, faculty, administrators, and community members to exchange comment and criticism on current issues. The paper should interpret international and national events for its readers and show how these events affect their lives. It should present and clarify the school's goals and values and serve as an entertainment medium, giving its readers casual diversion and enjoyment.

Obviously, student publications have a large role to play. Some school papers rival professional publications in content and format; others have difficulty in progressing beyond an elementary stage. Most do a commendable job. However, the success of a student publication often depends on the attitudes of student journalists on the staff.

Call it the "you" factor, because your attitude will determine not only if you will succeed in scholastic journalism but whether the publication you work on will be successful. Enthusiasm, a willingness to learn and work, the determination to do more than get by, and the ability to work with others—all are factors for success in any area. In short, journalism is like any other undertaking: You'll get out of it exactly what you put into it.

Assignment 1

Determine what you think should be the purpose of a school newspaper. On a separate piece of paper, rank the following statements from 1 to 5—1 meaning "very important," 2 meaning "important," 3 meaning "average," 4 meaning "of little importance," and 5 meaning "of no importance"—then discuss your ratings with your classmates.

The student newspaper should:

1. Report school news.

2. Report community news.

3. Report national and international news.

4. Present editorials on student matters.

5. Present editorials on community matters.

6. Present editorials on national and international matters.

7. Serve as a forum for student opinion.

8. Serve as a forum for faculty and administration opinion.

9. Serve as a forum for anyone who wishes to state an opinion.

10. Present interesting articles about students.

11. Present interesting articles about faculty and administrators.

12. Present interesting articles about people who have no connection with the school.

13. Serve as a publicity outlet for school activities.

14. Serve as an informational outlet for administrators and faculty to the students.

15. Serve as a newsletter for parents and other interested persons.

16. Provide journalistic experience and training for students.

17. Provide opportunities for the staff and adviser to win awards and recognition.

18. Provide a way to raise money by selling newspapers and advertising.

Assignment 2

Use the same rating system from Assignment 1 to rank the following groups of people. Determine whose opinions and ideas should be represented in the school newspaper and then discuss your rankings with your classmates.

1. Students

2. Faculty

3. Administrators

4. Newspaper adviser

5. Advertisers

6. Parents

7. Community members

Assignment 3

Using the same rating system and the same groups from Assignment 2, determine what readers the newspaper should try to reach. Discuss your rankings with your classmates.

Assignment 4   Review several past issues of your school newspaper to determine how well it is fulfilling its purpose as a student publication. Discuss your findings in class.

Summary

Journalism is an exciting career, and most professional journalists began their careers working on school publications. Even for those who do not pursue a career in journalism, studying journalism offers opportunities to develop writing and thinking skills and the ability to work with others. Scholastic journalism, at its best, reflects fully and meaningfully the people, events, and concerns of a particular school.

2 The Law, Standards, and Ethics

"Did you read that story in the school paper?"

"Yeah. I'll bet they're going to get in trouble over that!"

Are they? That's a good question. It depends on the attitude of school administrators toward student publications, and, perhaps most importantly, on the degree of professionalism shown by the students in their handling of the story. Student journalists, like professional writers, should follow a code of ethics that dictates a standard of professional conduct and be aware of the limitations to press freedom.

The History of Press Freedom

In 1735, John Peter Zenger, publisher of *The New York Weekly Journal,* was put on trial for "seditious libel." Zenger was charged with printing certain facts about Governor William Cosby that resulted in public criticism of the British governor. Whether or not the charges were true made no difference. In the mid-1700s, the fact that Zenger dared to print something unfavorable about the governor was considered proof of his guilt.

Zenger's attorney, Andrew Hamilton of Philadelphia, Pennsylvania, surprised the courtroom audience by admitting his client's guilt. However, he then appealed to the jury's concern for freedom and liberty and urged them to find Zenger not guilty. Hamilton asked the jury to lay "a noble foundation for securing to ourselves, our posterity, and our neighbors, that to which nature and the laws of our country have given us a right—the liberty both of exposing and opposing arbitrary power by speaking and writing—truth."

Hamilton's stirring appeal, and the jury's acquittal of Zenger, did indeed secure a "noble foundation" for journalism. It established the right of newspapers to print the truth, without fear of governmental punishment. The Zenger trial and a student newspaper's printing of stories dealing with controversial issues may seem to have little in common. However, there's an important question to consider: If Zenger could print the truth and not be punished, do student journalists have the same right?

Limitations to Press Freedom

The answer to that question is a qualified "yes." Prior to 1969, high-school students didn't have First Amendment rights. Parents generally thought of school administrators and teachers as their representatives, having the right to control their teenagers' lives while they were at school. This included the right to suppress student expression.

A change came when the United States Supreme Court ruled that public high-school students are entitled to the protection of the First Amendment. In the case of *Tinker v. Des Moines Independent Community School District,* three students said that school officials violated their First Amendment right to free expression when they were suspended for wearing black armbands to express mourning for people killed in the Vietnam War.

"First Amendment rights, applied in the light of the special characteristics of the school environment, are available to teachers and students," the Court said. "It can hardly be argued that either students or teachers shed their constitutional rights to freedom of speech or expression at the schoolhouse gate."

In addition to ruling that public students have First Amendment rights (including freedom of the press), the Supreme Court ruled in the case of *Southeastern Promotions, Ltd. v. Conrad,* in 1975, that once the state has established a forum through which public expression can take place, the state cannot practice prior restraint. That is, it cannot censor or stop expression in that forum, unless it is specifically illegal.

Known as the **Forum Theory,** it was interpreted in court cases until 1988 that public high school administrators did not have the unrestricted right to control the content of student publications. Even if a publication were sponsored and funded by a school district, the courts held that this did not make school administrators owners of the publication and did not give them the right to censor.

Principles for Avoiding Libel

But does this mean student newspapers can print anything they wish? The answer is no. Student publications operate under the same restrictions as the professional press. They are prohibited from printing libel, unjustly harming someone's reputation. Also, they are not allowed to print obscenity, and, in the case of scholastic publications, anything that could cause a substantial disruption of the educational process.

In addition, publications cannot print articles that invade a person's privacy, could incite a riot, or threaten national security. Nor can they advertise an illegal product or service. Further, a publication cannot print material written by another person without giving credit to that person, nor can it reprint copyrighted material without written permission. This is plagiarism.

Libel is published information that is false. In order to prove libel, the person harmed must show that:

1. The information is false.

2. It was communicated to a third party.

3. It refers to and reflects on a specific individual or on his or her business or product.

4. It damages that person's reputation or business in the eyes of the community.

5. It is the result of negligence on the part of the reporter or publication publishing the information.

In addition, in the case of public figures, it must be proved that the information was published with malice. In other words, published with intent to harm.

Restrictions in Student Publications

To date, no student publication has been legally judged obscene, nor has there been a single reported court decision in which someone has won a libel action against a school for something a student newspaper printed.

The same court decisions that have given students First Amendment rights have also given administrators the right to halt any expression that could cause a "substantial disruption of, or material interference with" school activities. In addition, the 1988 Supreme Court decision in the case of *Hazelwood School District v. Kuhlmeier* gave administrators the right to exercise "editorial control over the style and content of student speech in school-sponsored activities, so long as their actions are reasonably related to legitimate pedagogical concerns."

Some administrators have interpreted this to mean they can halt the publication of any article they're uncomfortable with, on grounds that it's not part of the "lessons the activity is designed to teach."

Since that time, however, several states, including Arkansas, California, Colorado, Iowa, Kansas, and Massachusetts, have enacted legislation which returns to students the First Amendment rights they lost in the *Hazelwood* decision. In addition, the *Hazelwood* case has prompted several publications' staffs to draw up comprehensive publications policies which guarantee a free student press, while spelling out corresponding responsibilities.

Assignment 1

Determine the legality or ethics of the following situations. Be prepared to discuss your opinions in class.

1. Student journalists want to distribute in several classes a survey on student alcohol consumption. The results will be used without names in a story in the student newspaper. The principal refuses to allow this, explaining

that school policy prohibits distribution of nonsubject-related question-naires in classes. Should she do that?

2. An editorial in the student newspaper criticizes the principal for refusing to allow distribution of the questionnaire. When the principal learns of the editorial, she refuses to allow the newspaper to be distributed. Do you agree with her?

3. A student newspaper editor wants to run a story in which an unnamed student is quoted as saying the principal is "a real stupid jerk who can't put her pants on without help." The adviser tells the editor not to print this, but she wants to print it anyway. With whom do you agree?

4. A newspaper columnist reports that Modine Gunch and Winston Cavitie were seen at the drive-in movie and were so busy steaming up the car windows that they didn't know what movie was showing. Should the editor print this?

5. A distraught student threatens to commit suicide by jumping off the roof of the school but is talked out of it by a teacher. The student newspaper editor runs a story about the incident with the student's name and a picture of him on the roof. Was she right in doing this?

6. A student writes a letter to the editor in which he makes racial slurs against minorities. The editor wants to print the letter. Should he do so?

7. A former student is interviewed after being arrested for armed robbery. The story contains several obscenities that reflect the student's anger and frustration. The editor prints the story and the obscenities. What would you have done?

Operating under First Amendment Rights

Many administrators work with students and advisers in establishing responsible publications policies that allow student journalists the First Amendment rights guaranteed by the Constitution. In most school publications, an adviser is in charge of the program.

Another common practice is to give authority of a publication to a publications board. The adviser, an administrator, and the publications staff usually form the board. It has the responsibility for overseeing the implementation of a publications and editorial policy. Other responsibilities may be added as needed. For example, the board might be charged with reviewing and making disciplinary recommendations for a violation of policy, ethics, or standards.

A publications board might also be made up of the publication's editors, the adviser, an administrator, teachers, parents, representatives of the professional press, and students who aren't involved in the publications program. The board's purpose would be to approve publication and editorial policies and review complaints and violations of the policies.

A publications policy sets guidelines for how the publications will be produced and distributed. An editorial policy describes the publication's editorial purpose and sets standards for staff members. Examples of publication and editorial policies can be found in the appendix.

Allowing Private Persons Their Privacy

Establishing a publications board and defining editorial policies can head off potential problems. Informing students about the board and policies also lets readers know what they can expect from the publications.

Some people are pleased to see their names or pictures in the paper, but others think this invades their privacy. Because of their occupations and newsworthiness, public officials and public figures give up much of their claim to privacy.

Private figures, however, are entitled to a life free from intrusion by the press, except in a newsworthy situation. Basically, publications are prohibited from publishing private—even though truthful—information about such people without their consent. Nor can they use people's names or pictures in an advertisement without their permission.

On the other hand, it's permissible to write about, and picture, people involved in an accident without their permission, because they're part of a newsworthy event. Students' quotations can be used in a student publication without their permission, provided they know they are being interviewed for a story. By agreeing to talk to a reporter, it's assumed they are giving the reporter permission to use the information.

Assignment 2

You are the editor of the student newspaper. In the following situations, determine what you would do; then share your decisions and your reasons with the class.

1. While talking with the principal, she tells you that because of discipline problems off-campus during lunch, she plans to ask the school board to close the campus for lunchtime. Students would have to eat lunch in the cafeteria. She then tells you the information is "off the record," and that you can't print it until after the school board meeting next month. What would you do?

2. Several members of the championship tennis team tell you they are quitting because the coach is playing favorites and benching some of the top players because he doesn't like their parents. The coach refuses to talk to your reporter, who has written the story without his comments. If the story is to be in the next issue of the newspaper, you must turn it in tonight. What would you do?

3. You've just published a story quoting an unidentified student who admits to selling drugs on campus. The principal calls you into his office, introduces you to two police officers, and then asks you to give them the name of the student drug pusher for arrest and questioning. What should you do?

4. The vice principal in charge of academics comes into your room while you're working on the newspaper and hands you a list of names. It's a list of 400 students who have made the Dean's Honor Roll, and she tells you she wants you to publish the list on the front page of the next issue. What would you do?

5. Your best writer has turned in an excellent feature story about cheating on exams. You learn that she created some of the quotes and attributed them to others. In addition, you suspect she made up some of the facts in the story. She's excited about having the story printed so she can enter it in a state journalism contest. What would you do?

6. Each issue of your newspaper carries a student review of one or two nearby eating establishments that are frequented by students. For this issue, the review is about a pizzeria that happens to be your biggest advertiser. Although the review is fair and accurate, it's unflattering and is sure to hurt the restaurant's business. The owners very likely would cancel their advertising. What would you do?

7. A reporter comes to you with a story about a social studies teacher who is disliked by many students. The story explains that the teacher is quite forgetful in class, is often absent, and rarely teaches, relying instead on students reading the textbook aloud in class. Even other teachers appear not to respect this teacher. The story then reveals that the teacher was once treated for a mental illness. Would you print the story?

Earning Confidence through Accuracy and Fairness

Now that you've learned what student publications can and cannot legally print, take a look at what they should and shouldn't print. More specifically, to what standards and ethics should publications and journalists subscribe?

The basic responsibility of a publication is to serve the public by disseminating news, information, and thoughtful opinion; yet this must be done in such a way that the publication maintains the credibility of its readers. Credibility—the public's confidence in the information in a publication—is gained through accuracy, objectivity, and fairness.

Responsible journalists check and double-check all facts. They make sure every name is spelled correctly, that information presented is factual, that opinion is presented as such, and that quotes are precisely what a person has said.

The pressure of a deadline should never prevent a journalist from turning in an accurate story. No publication or journalist is perfect, however, and sometimes mistakes appear. It's important to keep such mistakes to a minimum, and when they do occur, to correct them as soon as possible.

Maintaining Objectivity

People are entitled to hold opinions, and that includes journalists and their publications. However, responsible journalists limit opinion to their editorials and to columns and keep their opinions out of their news stories.

Readers are quick to spot slanted stories, and just as quickly they can judge a reporter or publication as prejudiced and not to be taken seriously. A good rule for maintaining objectivity is to report precisely what happened and exactly what people said, then let the readers form their own opinions.

The best formula for maintaining fairness as a journalist is still The Golden Rule. By treating others as you would like to be treated, you can avoid bad feelings. This concept of fair play can be applied to all levels of journalism—from making appointments for interviews, to presenting all viewpoints in a story fairly, clearly, and openly, and to avoiding reporting only sensational or controversial aspects of a story.

Following a Code of Ethics

The leading student publications have a stated purpose and a written set of standards. Likewise, thoughtful student journalists have a written code of ethics. When publications and journalists have guidelines to follow, they know what's expected of them and try to meet those standards.

A publication's editorial policy usually consists of a statement of purpose, school or district policy about student publications, a definition of the publication's audience, a listing of editorial goals the publication hopes to achieve, and a brief description of legal and editorial freedoms and responsibilities.

Some editorial policies are comprehensive and detailed, and others are very brief. Each publication staff determines what's most appropriate for its situation.

An editorial policy is like a road map. Once the staff members gain a strong sense of purpose and determine where they are and where they want to go, an exciting journey can begin.

Assignment 3

Using as a model the code of ethics for professional journalists in the appendix, develop a list of ethics for reporters and a set of standards for a student newspaper.

Assignment 4

If your student newspaper has an editorial policy, obtain a copy and see how it compares with the same policies printed in the appendix. Discuss what changes you would make.

Assignment 5

Using the examples of publication guidelines found in the appendix, draw up a proposed set of guidelines for your school publication. Discuss them in class.

Summary

The trial of John Peter Zenger in 1735 established truth as a defense for publishing facts and set the stage for press freedom in America. It wasn't until 1969, however, that First Amendment rights were extended to public high-school students through the United States Supreme Court's decision in *Tinker v. Des Moines Independent Community School District.*

Those rights were restrained by the Court in 1988 in the case of *Hazelwood School District v. Kuhlmeier,* when the Court said school administrators could exercise editorial control over student expression, including publications, so long as that control is reasonably related to educational concerns.

Under First Amendment rights, student publications are prohibited from printing libel, obscenity, or anything that would substantially disrupt the educational process. Nor can they print material that invades a person's privacy, could incite a riot, or threaten national security. Also, student publications cannot advertise illegal products or services or plagiarize or violate copyright laws.

Many student publications operate without administrative editorial control because they have developed and followed a set of publication standards and ethics. The staffs of these publications have publication boards, along with their own personal standards and ethics. They have established a reputation for professionalism and credibility by stressing accuracy, objectivity, and fairness in all they do.

3 News and News Leads

Think for a minute: Exactly what is news? Can you describe it? One dictionary defines news as "a recent event or happening, especially one that is unusual or notable." Another says news is "information about events that have just taken place, as reported regularly in a newspaper."

Apparently, then, news is something that has just happened. It must be unusual or notable, and it must appear in a newspaper or be broadcast on radio or television. But is that all? Let's find a better definition.

Most importantly, news must be factual. That means gossip and rumors aren't news. At the same time, facts alone aren't news. In order for facts to be considered news, they must concern something recent, and be of interest to a large number of people. So news is recent facts which are interesting to an audience. Even with this definition, though, there's more to newswriting than reporting interesting facts to readers.

Qualities of Newswriting

Newswriting has six qualities that distinguish it from other forms of writing. Newswriting deals with recent events, is accurate, objective, balanced, concise, and clear.

The term *recent* has a variety of meanings. The saying, "nothing's older than yesterday's news," is true for radio or television news broadcasting and daily newspapers. In the case of a biweekly or monthly school newspaper, however, yesterday's news might still be considered "hot." After an event is more than a week or ten days old, though, it is generally considered "old news" and should not be handled as a straight news story. Rather, it should be treated as a feature, a technique you'll learn in Chapter 8.

Another characteristic of a news story is accuracy. If errors and inaccuracies appear in a news story, the story is unbelievable and nonfactual, and credibility is lost. Fiction writers can be inaccurate and get away with it; newswriters cannot.

Objectivity means reporting facts without bias or prejudice, allowing the reader to determine their relative importance. Except in a column or an editorial, you should never interpret facts for readers, nor should your opinion be included in the story. Let the event and the facts speak for themselves.

When witnesses are sworn in to testify in court, part of the oath they take is to tell "the truth, the whole truth, and nothing but the truth." That's a good rule for newswriters to follow, especially in achieving story balance. Usually, there is more than one side to a story. Even a simple auto accident can produce more than one version of what happened. In newswriting, it is essential to give all major participants the opportunity for their views to be represented. Furthermore, these views must be presented accurately and fairly.

Newswriting should be clear and concise. The facts are presented in as few words as possible, without sacrificing necessary detail, and the language is easy to understand. Rather than dealing with complex words and phrases, sentences are constructed in subject-verb-object format, although simple phrases are often added for variety.

Because of these six qualities, newswriting is considered to be one of the best forms of written communication.

Making News Interesting

In addition to presenting facts that are recent, accurate, objective, balanced, clear, and concise, a major responsibility of the newswriter is to make sure the facts are interesting. Many elements make news interesting to an audience, but the most common ones are timeliness, proximity, consequence, prominence, drama, oddity, emotion, and conflict.

Timeliness deals with how soon an event has occurred or will occur when it is reported, while **proximity** refers to the nearness of an event to the audience. Proximity for a school newspaper can refer to physical distance— a fire that burns down a house in the next block—or to emotional distance— a local student wins a national speech contest in another state.

Consequence refers to the impact an event has on the readers, such as the effect a thirty-percent cut in school funding would have on class size. **Prominence** refers to readers' familiarity with a person in the news. A story concerning the principal's reaction to a budget cut would carry more interest than one built around a transfer student's comments.

The importance of next week's championship football game could be a source of **drama** in a news story, and the story of a girl trying out for the boys' basketball team would have the element of **oddity.** Reporting the death of a student in a weekend auto accident would be a highly **emotional** story. Charges of cheating brought by the losing candidate in a Student Council election might be the basis for a story of **conflict.**

There are other elements that make facts interesting to readers. Keep in mind that newsworthiness depends on how many elements are present in the story.

The story of a freshman who has the largest baseball-card collection in the state might be of interest to your readers because of proximity (he goes to your school) and oddity (few people have that many baseball cards). On the other hand, a story reporting student reaction to the school board's decision to save money by putting fifty or more students in every class would have a much higher degree of reader interest. That story would have proximity, consequence, prominence (quotes from school board members and well-known students), emotion, conflict, and perhaps other elements as well.

Understanding the nature of news and what makes news interesting is important, but equally important is the ability to write in a journalistic style. Newswriting isn't as difficult as it may seem. Anyone who has a basic grasp of the writing required in an English class can write news. The more you know about English and its usage, however, the easier newswriting will be. Many students find newswriting enjoyable and easier than other types of writing.

Assignment 1

You're the news editor of your high school newspaper. Decide which of the following stories you would print and then list the stories in order of priority. Discuss with the class the reasons for your rankings and why you would leave some stories, if any, out.

The principal will attend a Rotary Club luncheon next week as the special guest of the superintendent.

A famous rock star was injured last night during a concert in a neighboring state.

The student council has voted to spend $300 for prizes in a campus clean-up campaign.

The varsity golf team will compete for the district championship next week.

The governor has appointed your mayor to head his statewide reelection campaign.

The nearby pizza parlor is offering a two-for-one lunch special next month.

The star of a television series will be in town next week to speak on behalf of a charity drive.

The school board voted last night to extend the school day another hour, beginning next month.

A freshman at a rival school is seriously injured in an auto accident.

A junior at your school wins a speech contest in Washington, D.C.

An English teacher at your school won third place in a flower show over the weekend.

The home economics department will start a child-care service next week for students with children.

A plane crash in a neighboring state killed 128 people last night. None were from your town.

The football coach has benched a substitute player for two weeks for "goofing off" during practice.

The President announced this morning that he would veto the proposed budget approved by Congress last night.

The drama department has announced the play and cast for next month's musical production.

Six Basic News Questions

Because news is based upon facts, it is up to you as the newswriter to have the facts available before you begin writing. In gathering facts, the reporter must ask questions that, in essence, are based upon the **Five Ws and H: Who, What, When, Where, Why,** and **How.** However, newswriting for the 21st century must have more than the "bare facts." In order to keep reader attention and tell the complete story, the reporter must include information that helps give readers the "feel" as well as the facts of a story. This information comes from asking more **"How"** and **"Why"** questions, as well as getting your news sources' opinions and feelings on the subject of your story. But how do you present these facts, and how do you begin the story?

The newswriter should be a storyteller, using the facts to narrate the story in an interesting and informative manner. This means that before you begin writing, you need to decide the importance of each fact and what supportive information will help the reader better understand that importance. You'll also need to determine which facts and supporting information will be used and which ones will be discarded. You can then arrange the facts and information in the best storytelling form, usually in descending order of importance and interest. Sound tough? It isn't, really, if you start at the beginning.

The most important part of a news story is the beginning, which is referred to as the **lead.** A news story lead does two things: It gives the reader an idea what the story is about, and it gets the reader interested in continuing through the rest of the story. This means the writer must ask two questions: "What is this story really about?" and "What is the best way to explain that to the reader?"

Assume you've just come from a student council meeting. The meeting opened with the Pledge of Allegiance. The minutes of the last meeting were read and approved, and the president called for the treasurer's report. After the treasurer reported that $300 was made at the dance last week, the president called for old business, but there was none. Under new business, a member suggested that part of the dance money be used as prize money for competition between classes to clean up the campus. After some discussion, the motion was approved, and the meeting was adjourned.

Now you are going to write the story for your school paper. What is the story about? Is it about the fact the student council held a meeting? No! The results of the meeting, like the results of a vote or an athletic event, are always more important than the fact that a meeting, election, or athletic event was held. What happened at the meeting? The Pledge of Allegiance and the reading of the minutes took place, but these events hold no interest for your readers, nor are these routine actions important. Two matters of interest and importance took place at the meeting. The treasurer reported that last week's dance earned $300 for the council, and members voted to use part of the money to initiate a campus clean-up campaign. Your lead, then, could deal with the money earned from the dance and explain how it will be used. Or it could portray an imaginary scene depicting an activity on Clean-up Day. The story would continue with further details about the money and clean-up campaign, followed by quotations from the president, treasurer, or some council members concerning the dance proceeds and campaign plans, as well as details of both.

Breaking the Story Idea into Components

One of the simplest ways to construct the lead for a news story is to ask first what the story is really about and then to break the main story idea into the basic **Five Ws** and **H** components. WHO is the story about, or WHO is the principal person or organization? WHAT has happened, or WHAT will happen? WHEN did, or WHEN will the event happen? WHERE did, or WHERE will the event happen? WHY did, or WHY will this event happen? HOW did, or HOW will this event happen?

After breaking the story idea into components, try each of the parts as a lead for your story. Although most professional news stories follow the who-did-what pattern, leading with the "why" or "how" will usually prove to be of greater reader interest because such an introduction tells them, in an interesting way, why the story is important. You can often determine which lead is best by reading each one aloud. The one that sounds best to you will probably be a good lead.

In addition to using component leads, there are other ways to begin a news story. For example, you might try one of the following grammatical leads. Notice how each lead sets the tone for the story:

Noun Lead:	A clean campus may be the result of a recent student council dance.
Verb Lead:	Cleaning up the campus is the next target for student council action.
Prepositional Phrase Lead:	After a successful dance, the student council has voted to clean up the campus.
Casual Clause Lead:	Because last week's dance was a financial success, a cleaner campus may be coming.
Conditional Clause Lead:	If the student council gets its way, the campus will soon be cleaner.
Past Participle Lead:	Spurred on by the success of its recent dance, the student council will take on campus clutter next.
Present Participle Lead:	Raising $300 at its dance last week, the student council is planning a campus clean-up campaign.
Question Lead:	Would you be willing to help clean up the campus for a chance at 300 bucks?

Picture Lead: Picking up what must have been his five-hundredth piece of trash, the senior football player straightened up and wondered silently, "Why am I doing this?" The answer came quickly: "For the money? Naw. For the pride of the senior class!"

Assignment 2

Look through your local newspaper and find ten news leads you like. Bring them to class and tell why you like them. See if you can find the **Five Ws** and **H** in each lead.

Assignment 3

Use the following facts to find the main idea in each story; then break it into the **Five Ws** and **H.** Write a news lead for each story. It isn't necessary to write more than a sentence or two.

1. The PTA met last night in the cafeteria.

   Treasurer Inez Martinez reported there are 152 members, and that the treasury has $863.

   President Wilson Wong presented several awards.

   Government teacher Celia Starbuck was named "Teacher of the Year" for her work with the Homework Hotline.

   Member Kathy Burrows was named "Member of the Year" for having perfect attendance.

   The meeting started at 7:30 P.M. and ended at 9:45 P.M. A total of seventy-eight members attended.

2. Transfer student Joe Platto was killed yesterday in an automobile accident.

   Platto was driving south on Waits Street when another car apparently ran a stop sign at the intersection with Chambers Avenue and broadsided Platto's car.

   Platto was driving a blue 1995 Corolla. It was demolished.

   Sergi Clements, 34, was driving the other car, a 1989 Buick.

   Clements wasn't hurt, but his car received an estimated $800 worth of damage.

   Clements was ticketed for running a stop sign and for reckless driving.

   Platto was rushed to Mercy Hospital by EMS, where he died without regaining consciousness.

   Funeral services will be held the day after tomorrow at 3:00 P.M., at Rose Funeral Home. Burial will follow at Perpetual Rest Cemetery.

   Students with written parental permission will be allowed to miss after-noon classes to attend the services.

   A special memorial service will be held in the gym, before school starts, the day after tomorrow.

Writing Strong News Leads

There are many ways to lead a news story, but the purpose remains the same—to give the reader an idea of what the story is about and to do it in an interesting manner. There are, however, a number of techniques for writing a news lead that have proven to be effective.

The first technique is to keep the lead sentence to twenty-five or thirty words, if possible, and the opening paragraph to one or two sentences. To help keep the lead brief and draw in the reader, use only the most important of the **Five Ws** and **H** in your lead. Save the rest for later in the story. Also, try to get the most interesting fact of the story into the first few words of the lead.

The second technique is to establish the tone of your story in the lead. If it's to be a humorous news story, be humorous in the lead.

The third technique is to use strong, active verbs in your lead. Avoid using the passive voice: "A dance will be held by the student council." Use present and future tense whenever possible: "The student council will hold a dance." Active verbs and present tense help make the story seem current and important.

Another technique for good leads is to create a question in the reader's mind: "Overlooking a newly created holiday will cause the Lions to be the visiting team for the Homecoming game." To understand this, readers will be compelled to read further. Raising a question isn't the same as actually asking one. Whenever possible, avoid using a question lead, unless it is a compelling one: "How would you like to have a new car?" Also, avoid a quotation lead, unless it is a strong quote that can stand on its own: "I've got a gun in your back. Now do exactly as I say."

A final time-proven technique is to write three different leads for your story and the pick the one that sounds best. Chances are, one of the leads will be a clunker, one will seem fair, and the third will be a powerful one.

Most newswriters agree that the hardest part of writing is getting started. By learning different types of leads, by reading leads in magazines and newspapers, and by actually writing leads, you'll find getting started will become easier. Then, with a good beginning, you'll discover that your news story can be written quickly. And chances are, it will be good, too.

Assignment 4

Read the following information; then follow the instructions given below.

The Cedarville School Board met at 7:30 P.M. Monday in the board room.

It was a regular bimonthly meeting.

Board members heard an administrative report listing several instances of students leaving campus during lunch, smoking cigarettes, drinking alcoholic beverages, and taking various kinds of drugs.

After hearing the report, board members voted to eliminate the off-campus lunch program for students beginning with the next school year.

The vote, by a show of hands, was unanimous.

1. Write a news lead using each of the **Five Ws** and **H** (a total of six leads) for the information above. Select the two you like best and share them with the class.

2. Select five of the examples of grammatical leads given in this chapter and use them with the Cedarville School Board information to write news leads. Select the two you like best and discuss them with the class.

Assignment 5   Select four stories from the last issue of your school newspaper. Write at least three leads for each story. Share with the class the one you like best for each story.

Summary

Newswriting is the art of presenting facts that are of interest to a group of readers. It differs from other forms of writing in that it concerns something recent and is accurate, objective, balanced, concise, and clear. While a statement of mere facts can be dull, newswriting creates and holds reader interest through timeliness, proximity, consequence, prominence, drama, oddity, emotion, and conflict. A good newswriter is a good storyteller. That is why many students find newswriting an enjoyable form of writing.

Before newswriting can begin, facts and information that will help the reader gain a "feel" for the story must be gathered. Journalists obtain information by asking many questions. The basic questions they ask are *who, what, when, where, why,* and *how*. The facts received are then presented in an interesting and informative manner, usually in order of importance, with supportive information to help the reader better understand the importance of those facts. Newswriters give readers an idea of what the story is about in the first paragraph, or lead, of the story and then develop the story in succeeding paragraphs. The lead also entices readers to continue reading. That's why the lead is the most important part of a news story.

4 Writing the News

One of the biggest problems with scholastic newswriting is that many stories fall apart after the lead. The lead can be excellent, causing the reader to want more information. If the body of the story is disorganized, however, the reader becomes confused and moves on to another story, or even worse, the reader may discard the publication without reading the other stories.

As mentioned earlier, the lead is the most important part of the story, but the rest of the story must also be written in a clear, concise, and easy-to-read style. To do this, a journalist must build a sound story structure by using facts and supporting information in a logical sequence, adding quotations to lend credibility to the facts and information, and using transitions to provide continuity and smoothness.

The basis of the story structure begins before the journalist puts the first word on paper or the computer. After determining the focus of the story and selecting the lead, the journalist must arrange the facts in the best storytelling form, as described in the previous chapter.

For beginning newswriters, it often helps, especially with a complex story, to arrange facts in an outline form. Identify the major points of the story and, using key words, jot them down in order of importance. Next take the supporting facts and quotes and place them in the outline beneath the major points where they most logically fit. In most cases, the story should not be written in chronological order. Rather, it should consist of a set of logically related facts that are connected by supportive quotes and held together with transitions.

This exercise is designed to help you read through a set of facts to find a lead and then group those facts to write a story. Put an *l* in front of the sentence you think contains lead information. If there is another sentence you think also belongs in the lead, put an *l* in front of it, too. Next group sentences of information that logically go together in a paragraph and number them. When you've completed that step, arrange your groups of information in order of importance. Discard those that are unimportant. Then write a story.

1. _____ President Bill Bates opened the meeting at 1:07 P.M. on Monday, February 13.

_____ Twenty-three council members were present; twelve were absent.

_____ Junior Suzy Forester led the Pledge of Allegiance.

_____ Senior Wilma Johnson read the minutes of the last meeting for senior Trudy Dodson, who was absent.

_____ Junior Henry Wu, treasurer, reported that council income for the month was $317, and expenditures were $43, leaving a balance of $482.

_____ Under old business, Bates asked junior Freddie Sanchez, dance chairman, to give a report on the council dance, held last Saturday.

_____ Sanchez reported that more than 300 people attended the dance; $390 was made form admissions; $60 was made on refreshments; the DJ cost $150. Total profit was $300.

_____ "It's the best dance we've had this year. Everybody had a great time. They're still talking about it today," Sanchez said.

_____ "You and your committee did a great job, Freddie. Ms. Elmhurst (Principal Molly Elmhurst) said she thought it was the best-run dance she'd ever seen. Tell everybody thanks," Bates said.

_____ "What are we going to do with all that money?" freshman Will Brown asked.

_____ "That's a good question," Bates said, then asked for suggestions from the floor.

_____ Senior Lester Charles suggested a student council party.

_____ Sophomore Wendi Wardlow suggested buying flowers and shrubs and planting them in front of the school.

_____ "That's a waste of money. This school is so trashed already; nobody would be able to see the flowers anyway," junior Travis Peters said.

_____ "Why don't we have a contest to clean up the school and give prizes to the people who do the best job," freshman Joe Dexter suggested.

_____ After further discussion, Dexter moved and Wardlow seconded a motion to conduct a Clean Campus Weekend on Saturday, March 11, and award $150 to the class that collected the most trash, with $75 going to the second-place class. The motion was approved.

_____ Bates appointed Dexter to head up the Clean Campus Committee and be in charge of the contest.

_____ "I'm sure Joe and his committee will do a great job, but I'm also sure the seniors will prevail," Bates said.

_____ There being no further business, the meeting was adjourned at 1:43 P.M.

Now it's your turn. Find the lead and group the information on your own. Then write the story. Assume you're writing the story for the *Cedarville High Press,* which will be distributed to students on Friday.

2. _____ The Cedarville School Board met at 7:30 P.M. on Monday in the board room.

_____ After a reading of the minutes, the board heard Ms. Ann Washington's request to waive the board's 30-day ineligibility rule for out-of-district transfer students, so that her son, Henry, could begin playing football immediately.

_____ After discussion and questioning of Ms. Washington and Coach Alton Brewster, the board voted to postpone a decision until its next meeting.

_____ The board voted to accept the resignation "with regret" of English teacher Peggy Pierce, who is retiring after 41 years of service to the district.

_____ "Miss Pierce is Cedarville High School as far as I'm concerned. Practically every member of this board was a student of hers, including me. She is one of the finest English teachers in the nation, and I know we are going to miss her and her talents immensely," board president Samuel Martinez said.

_____ Certificates of Honor were presented to Johnny Meister for winning the county spelling bee contest; to Darla Chambers for placing third in the physics division of the state high-school science fair; and to Yang Su Chin for being named the top high school photographer in the state.

_____ Mrs. Thelma Carpenter, president of the Cedarville Parent–Teacher Association, presented a report on the association's national Drug Awareness Week campaign. She asked the board to declare the week of October 17–23 as Drug Awareness Week in all Cedarville schools.

_____ "Although drug and alcohol abuse doesn't seem to be as much of a problem in Cedarville as in other areas, it does exist here. We think by publicizing the bad effects of alcohol and drug abuse during Drug Awareness Week, we can encourage young people to resist drugs and alcohol and inspire them to help their friends who have a problem. If we don't take an active role in fighting this problem now, it will only get worse," Mrs. Carpenter said.

_____ After a brief discussion, the board approved the measure.

_____ The board voted to approve the purchase of $2,483 of athletic uniforms and equipment for the boys' basketball and girls' softball programs.

_____ "I'm tired of being ashamed of the way our kids look out on the court or on the field. There's no sense in our kids looking ragtag. They're representing Cedarville and should look as good as the football team or the other teams in the district," board member Sidney White said.

_____ The board voted to approve a 45-day extension for Simpco Company to pay their school taxes.

_____ "They've been doing business here for 23 years and times are tight right now. I think we can afford to help them out a little," board vice-president Gale Starnes said.

_____ Cedarville High Principal Molly Elmhurst proposed that the board adopt a policy that would bar from all extracurricular activities those students caught selling, using, or buying drugs or alcohol. Under the proposal, student violators would be excluded from extracurricular activities for the rest of the semester. A second violation would exclude them from activities for the remainder of the school year and would deny them any awards they might have won. They would also be required to participate in a counseling program on the dangers of drug and alcohol use.

_____ "I think we should do whatever we can to stop alcohol and drug abuse by our students. Extracurricular activities are a privilege, not a right, and we should hold students to higher standards if they wish to participate in these activities. This isn't a radical new idea. Many school districts throughout the nation have success-fully implemented this kind of program. I agree with what Mrs. Carpenter said earlier. We don't have a major drug or alcohol problem yet, but I want to make sure we don't ever have one," Ms. Elmhurst said.

_____ "We've had a similar policy for our kids for two years, and it has worked very well. Athletes are required to sign an 'athletic contract' before the beginning of the season. The contract covers athletes using, selling, or possessing drugs or alcohol. The pen-alties include suspensions and referrals to abuse education pro-grams in the school. In two years, I've had to enforce the penalties only once," Coach Brewster said.

_____ "We met with Ms. Elmhurst prior to this meeting tonight, and although we agree with the purpose of the proposal, we do not believe it will eliminate the drug and alcohol problem. Frankly, many of the problem students are not involved in extracurricular activities anyhow. We need a plan to deal with these students," Mrs. Carpenter said.

_____ "I think this proposal is absurd. It's the parents' responsibility to punish their kids for drug or alcohol abuse, not the school's. I think Ms. Elmhurst is trying to have the school replace the parent, and I don't think it has any right to do this. I agree that drug and alcohol abuse is a problem, but they're going about it in the wrong way. As Mrs. Carpenter said, the kids who have a drug and alcohol problem aren't involved in extracurricular activities anyhow. This proposal won't affect them. All it's going to do is cause a few kids to be a little more careful about using drugs and alcohol, that's all," senior class president Richard Dycus said.

_____ "I don't think this proposal goes far enough. As far as I'm concerned, all those drug-taking burnouts and boozers ought to be kicked out of school and run out of town. The real problem is the parents. They just let those kids run wild. Something ought to be done about the parents," Mrs. Emma Hargrove, a Cedarville resident, said.

_____ After a brief discussion, the board voted to take the proposal under advisement and to hold a public hearing at its next meeting in two weeks.

_____ The board voted to pay all routine bills for the month, adjourned the meeting, then went into executive session.

The LT-QT-QT Newswriting Method

Each news story should be written as the facts dictate, with the writer's experience and writing style determining how the facts will be presented. For beginning newswriters, there is a basic format that can help shape most news stories. It's called the **LT-QT-QT Newswriting Method.**

After writing the story lead, develop a second paragraph that contains information that further explains the information in the lead or further develops the storytelling style you've selected. This paragraph should be relatively short— just one or two sentences—and should lead into a quotation related to the subject of the lead. Here's an example:

> Picking up what must have been his five-hundredth piece of trash, the senior football player straightened up and wondered silently, "Why am I doing this?" The answer came quickly: "For the money? Naw. For the pride of the senior class."
>
> Student council members voted Monday to use part of the $300 raised at last week's dance as prize money for a campus clean-up campaign. According to council president Bill Bates, the money will

be given to the class that collects the most trash during Clean Campus Weekend, scheduled for Saturday, March 11.

"The winning class will receive $150, while the second-place class will receive $75," Bates, a senior, said. "I'm sure the seniors will lead the way."

After the lead paragraph (L) comes additional information that explains what the story is about and serves as a transition (T) from the descriptive, story-setting lead to the council president's quote. Professional journalists frequently refer to this second paragraph as the "nut graf"; it's the "nut" of the story. Following the council president's quote can be another paragraph that gives additional information and serves as a transition. Then comes another quote. This is the basis of the LT-QT-QT Newswriting Method.

In addition to simplifying the structure of a story, the LT-QT-QT Method encourages the writer to include several quotations. Quotes add drama to the facts, so that a reader will read the complete story and not quit after two or three paragraphs.

Direct and Indirect Quotes

There are two kinds of quotations—direct and indirect. Ordinarily, direct quotes are preferable, but indirect quotes are important, too. Direct quotes lend credibility to the story and are of more interest to readers. Readers would rather hear what people have to say than read what a reporter says they've said. Direct quotes should never repeat information already in the story, nor should they state the obvious.

Here's an example in which the quote in the second paragraph repeats information in the first paragraph:

A clean campus may be the result of a recent student council dance. Council members voted Monday to use part of the $300 raised at last week's dance as prize money for a campus clean-up campaign.

"We voted to use part of the $300 we raised at last week's dance as prize money for the clean-up campaign," council president Bill Bates said.

Here's an example of a quote stating the obvious:

According to Bates, the money will be given to the class that collects the most trash during Clean Campus Weekend, scheduled for Saturday, March 11.

"We hope the prize money will create competition between the classes," he said.

Direct quotations should be used for the following purposes:

1. Add credibility to the facts in a story.

2. Add interest and importance to a story by using a person's exact words.

3. Give the reader a feeling for unique speech patterns or drama that may have been apparent when the reporter gathered the information.

Indirect quotes are used to summarize long statements and serve as transitions from one set of facts to the next or from one direct quote to the next.

<table>
<tr><td>

Assignment 2

</td><td>

Refer to Assignment 3 in Chapter 3 on news and news leads. Take the two sets of information and write a complete news story for each.

</td></tr>
</table>

Attributing Quotations

Attribution tells the reader from whom the information was obtained. Both direct and indirect quotes, as well as most facts in a story, must be attributed to their source. After identifying the source in the story the first time, attribution can be handled by using "he said" or "she said." It is best to identify sources early in the story, and this identification should include first and last name and an accompanying title, such as principal, council president, parent, or sophomore. Then, quotes or facts can be attributed by using "he said" or "she said."

For example, refer to the first student council story in this chapter. Note that the first time Bill Bate's name is used, he's referred to as council president Bill Bates. Then, in the next paragraph, he's referred to as Bates, a senior. Thereafter, he would be referred to as Bates or "he."

Although all direct and indirect quotes must be attributed to their sources, not all facts need to be. If the facts are obvious, or have previously appeared in print, and contain no opinion or potential for controversy, they don't need attribution. But a newswriter should take this approach—when in doubt, attribute.

Usually attribution should come after the quote or fact. But in a long series of quotes or facts, the attribution can come after the first complete quote or statement of fact or be inserted at a natural break in the sentence.

> "The winning class will receive $150," Bates said, "while the second-place class will receive $75, but the other two classes won't receive anything."

The attribution in the example is placed at the first natural break in the quote, but it could also be placed in the second natural break, between "$75" and "but."

Other points to remember include beginning a new paragraph each time a new direct quote is used and each time the subject matter of the direct quote changes. You should never use the phrase "when asked" to lead into a quotation. Whether the quote was spontaneous or the result of a reporter's question is of no interest to the reader. All the reader want to know is *what* was said and *who* said it—in that order.

<table>
<tr><td>

Assignment 3

</td><td>

Refer to Assignment 4 in Chapter 3. Use one of the leads you've already developed, or write another lead based upon the information given in the activity. Then, using the following information—which are direct quotes—develop the rest of the story. You may use any information as either direct or indirect quotes. Assume you're writing the story for the Friday issue of *Cedarville High Press,* which will be distributed to students Friday morning.

</td></tr>
</table>

Samuel Martinez, School Board president:	I don't know why the school newspaper would be interested in something like this. After all, the town paper does a good job reporting on our meetings. However, you do a good job, too. I really liked that article you did on my wife's antique doll collection. That's the kind of good news I like to see in a school paper.
	Well, the off-campus lunch policy didn't seem to be working. From reports we received from administrators and teachers, students were returning late for classes. Many were coming back in various stages of intoxication or were high on drugs. We've had reports from downtown businesses of students loitering and shoplifting and littering their stores. Police chief Marvin Lancaster said kids are always speeding to and from school, trying to spend as much time out of school as possible.
	We thought it would be better for all parties if we closed the campus for lunch. I hope you agree with us and write an editorial supporting our decision.
Principal Molly Elmhurst:	I'm glad the board took the action it did. When the open-campus policy was instigated two years ago, we knew we'd have problems. We wanted to give students a break, but we never expected the number of problems nor the seriousness of the problems.
	The cafeteria is more than able to handle a full student load. Plus, we're planning to introduce a snack-food line and a salad bar next year. This will give students three lunch options. The policy will go into effect the first day of school next year.
	I know students will be upset with the decision, but it's for their own good.
Senior Bill Bates, student council president:	As usual, the administration is using one or two bad examples to justify cracking down on the entire student body. Sure, a few kids drink or smoke during lunch hours. A lot of teachers and administrators smoke during lunch hours, too. At any rate, why not try to deal with the problem-makers, rather than making problems for us all? I'm sure the council will want to do something about this, but right now I don't know what we can do to change the school board's mind. I plan to give a full report to the council at our next meeting, Friday at 1:30 P.M.

The Importance of Transitions

Facts and quotations are the building blocks of a news story, but **transitions** are the cement that hold the story together. By paying careful attention to the logical arrangement of facts and quotes in a story, a newswriter can construct a solid structure. In a logically assembled story, facts and quotes have transitional qualities that support each other in a natural sequence.

Transitions are words, phrases, clauses, sentences, or even paragraphs that help lead the reader from one idea or fact to the next. In some cases, transitions are key words in a paragraph that are repeated in a succeeding one. At other times, transition is achieved by referring to an idea or fact in the previous paragraph. Sometimes, a synonym can be used as a transitional device.

Often, transitions are individual words that are used to tie phrases, sentences, and paragraphs together to point the reader's direction through the story. A partial list of helpful transitions follows:

however	but	in the meantime	consequently
then	and	previously	furthermore
meanwhile	also	besides	on the other hand
later	thus	in addition	at the same time
additionally	or	for example	therefore
afterward	now	earlier	although

Let's see how transitions work in the student council story.

> A clean campus may be the result of a recent student council dance. Council members voted Monday to use part of the $300 raised at last week's dance as prize money for a campus clean-up campaign.
>
> According to council president Bill Bates, the money will be given to the class that collects the most trash during Clean Campus Week-end, scheduled for Saturday, March 11.
>
> "The winning class will receive $150, while the second-place class will receive $75," Bates, a senior, said. "I'm sure the seniors will lead the way."

Notice that the key words "clean," "campus," and "Council" are repeated in the second sentence of the first paragraph. These are key transitions. Also note how "council," "money," "class," and "Clean Campus" are key transitions from the first paragraph to the second paragraph. In addition, "the money" and "the class" in the second paragraph refer to facts in the first paragraph.

Again, "class" is used twice in the third paragraph as a transition from the second paragraph, while "$150" and "$75" are additional, specific bits of information in the third paragraph that also serve as synonyms for "money" in the first and second paragraphs. Serving as a transition from the first part of the quote to the second part is the word "senior." Individual word or phrase transitions include "according to" in the second paragraph and "while" in the third paragraph.

Transitions can be used in many ways to achieve coherence, and most beginning newswriters will discover they have a natural ability to use transitions because they use them when they talk to friends. This brings up an important secret of successful newswriting: Write the way you talk.

Readers want information presented in a clear, natural, and understandable way. As you outline the facts and quotes for your story, think how you would tell the story to a friend in a telephone conversation. Then write what you would say. Keep your language conversational, but avoid using first or second person whenever possible. Often, a way to test whether a sentence or paragraph will confuse a reader is to read it aloud to a friend. If it is confusing or doesn't sound right, then it probably needs to be rewritten.

You are a reporter for the Cedarville High School Press. From the following information, write a 250- to 300-word news story for your newspaper, which will be distributed to students Friday morning. You may use any statements attributed to individuals as direct quotes, or you may paraphrase them into indirect quotes, but do not change the meaning. Leave out any unnecessary details.

The Situation

Cedarville High received a telephone bomb threat at 2:30 P.M. Monday. Mrs. Anne Miles, senior secretary to Principal Molly Elmhurst, received the threat, consisting of a tersely worded statement: "A bomb has been planted in one of your lockers and has been programmed to detonate in less than thirty minutes. I suggest you abandon the school building immediately."

Miles relayed the message to Elmhurst, who ordered a quick evacuation of the building, and contacted police. A check of lockers by police bomb experts proved negative, and no device was found. The threat was a hoax. Police are investigating the case now, although Chief Marvin Lancaster admits no suspects have been taken into custody, and clues are few.

In order to avoid panic, school officials conducted the evacuation under the guise of a fire drill. It was the second drill in the past ten days and was conducted quickly and effectively, Elmhurst said.

Quotations

Mrs. Molly Elmhurst, principal:

If this was intended as a prank, you can be assured we're not taking it as such. This type of action is criminal, and we plan to file charges against the person or persons responsible.

I had just finished talking to Coach (Alton) Brewster when Mrs. Miles stepped into the office and quite calmly reported the bomb threat. As far as I know, we've never had a bomb threat here, and I was at first a bit confused as to what to do. It finally came to me to get everyone out of the building, and to call the police, which I did.

I think a few rounds of congratulations should go to the faculty and the students, who responded quickly and quietly to the evacuation. If there is a bright side to an incident like this, I suppose it's finding out that everyone is brushed up on their fire-drill procedures.

Chief Marvin Lancaster, Cedarville Police Department:

It will be difficult to break this case now, unless the culprit makes a stupid mistake by telling someone he or she did it, and then we find out about it. We were caught a bit offguard this time, but we won't be again.

I hope this isn't someone's idea of fun because he or she stands to get in quite a bit of trouble. Bomb threats are considered a Class A misdemeanor, and if convicted, the caller can be handed a maximum fine of $2,000, or one year in the county jail, or both.

It's a sad fact that schools are particularly susceptible to bomb threats. We have no system whereby we can actually protect the schools against such threats, but we've been extremely fortunate in that such threats are rare.

When a threat is received, the only thing we can do is evacuate the school, send two or three officers to investigate, and hope for the best.

These threats generally occur around test time, when kids haven't studied.

Ronald Clayton, junior and office aide: I was running off an office bulletin when the phone rang and Mrs. Miles answered it. She turned kind of pale all of a sudden, then hung up and walked quietly into the principal's office. I'd probably have fainted.

Wanda Jackson, sophomore: I'm really surprised this kind of thing doesn't happen more often, what with all the nuts running around in the world. I mean, a person knows that if he calls in a threat like that, he can disrupt the entire school. It's really kind of scary, if you think about it.

Additional Newswriting Tips

Although it's helpful to write the way you talk, some traits of oral language should be avoided. For example, don't use slang or clichés, and don't chat with the reader. Simply tell the facts as precisely and briefly as possible. Nor should opinion be used in writing a news story. Too often, beginning newswriters will combine slang, chichés, chattiness, and opinion in an effort to be known as a clever writer. Unfortunately, such writing comes across as juvenile.

"Jonathan Jones has been elected president of the newly organized Future Engineers Club" reads much better than, "There's a great new club at school! It's called the Future Engineers Club, and that well-liked senior, Jonathan Jones, is heading it up!"

Guidelines to keep in mind for writing news stories include:

1. Put the most interesting and important facts at the beginning of your story. If you use a Picture Lead, then your second paragraph should be a "nut graf," explaining the basic news of the story.

2. Write in the active voice. "The council awarded two cash prizes" reads better than, "Two cash prizes were awarded by the council."

3. Write in the third person.

4. Avoid tense changes. Most news stories are written in the past tense.

5. Keep sentences and paragraphs short. Whenever possible, use only one idea for each sentence. Set a maximum of twenty-five words for each sentence and one to three sentences for each paragraph. Use short, familiar words rather than long, unusual words.

6. Be specific. Use vivid, colorful words (especially verbs) and specific details, but avoid getting cute. Avoid vague adjectives such as *many, some, several,* and *few.*

7. Don't write over the reader's head, or insult the reader's intelligence by writing down. Give the reader whatever background is necessary to

understand the story, but do it briefly. Don't assume the reader will know what you're talking about.

8. Don't draw conclusions for your readers. Give them enough specific facts to reach their own conclusions.

9. Check and double-check spelling and grammar. Check and double-check the facts and quotes in your story. If in doubt about anything, check it out or leave it out. Also, double-check all names—first and last—against a directory.

At this point, you might think there is so much to remember that only a literary genius could write a compelling news story. Not true. Every day students are writing news stories that rival those found in the professional press. These students have become accomplished writers by learning the structure and mechanics of sound news writing and then applying them.

The way to become an accomplished news writer is to start writing news. It might seem difficult at first, but soon you'll notice an improvement, and you'll be on the road to becoming a polished news writer.

Summary

A news story needs more than a strong lead. The body of the story must be presented in a clear, concise, and easy-to-read manner. The structure of the story must be well-organized and should contain some direct quotes to hold reader interest. An excellent way to structure a news story is to alternate quotes with indirect quotes, facts, and transitions. Keep in mind that quotations, as well as many sets of facts, must be attributed to a source. Although there are many guidelines for writing professional-quality news, the best way to quickly master the technique is by actually writing news stories.

5 The Fine Art of Copyediting

The best journalists have secrets that help them remain at the top of their profession. In-depth research, skillful interviewing and note taking, and vivid writing are among their "trade secrets." Another factor is careful editing and rewriting. Copyediting is considered so important that most large newspapers pay copy editors more than reporters, and copy editors are considered to be above reporters in the management structure. Therefore, one of the secrets to being an excellent journalist is learning to edit copy. There's no better place to start than with your own news stories.

The tools of a copy editor include several sharpened pencils, a dictionary, a stylebook, a list of copyediting symbols, knowledge of the English language and its proper usage, and a passion for accuracy. Also helpful are a thesaurus, a student-faculty directory (if you're writing for a student publication), a list of newsworthy people and their titles, and a "morgue" of previous publications for checking background information.

Despite what you may have seen on television or in the movies, journalists aren't necessarily done when they've finished writing their stories. They go back through their stories, checking for content, structure, style, and errors. If only a few changes are required, they make them and then turn the stories over to the editor or file them in computer story banks. If there are major changes, they rewrite and edit them again.

The Magic Number 3

There's a curious phenomenon in the writing profession about rewriting. In discussing writing technique with freelance writers—those who sell their articles to publications on the basis of story appeal and writing ability—as well as with professional journalists and writing teachers, the number 3 keeps popping up. Many professional journalists say they usually write or compose at least three leads for a story, then select the best one.

In rewriting, many writers and journalists say their third story is the best. This third story is actually the second rewrite. These writers consider their first story a rough draft. They read through it and make content, structure, grammatical, and spelling corrections. Then they rewrite their story, making additional revisions as well as notations for other changes.

After editing their stories again, they rewrite a second time to produce a final version. Most agree that this is the best stopping point, because another revision may result in overwriting, which can dull a story considerably.

Reporters edit their own stories to produce the most accurate, well-written, and readable stories possible. This is also a task of the copy editor. Unfortunately, in too many instances, especially in schools, reporters and copy editors get caught up in details, missing the purpose of copyediting. Sometimes copyediting becomes a "me-versus-you" situation, instead of a cooperative "us" relationship.

The best copyediting situation occurs when reporters carefully edit their own copy—rewriting if necessary—and then give it to a copy editor who helps them turn the story into an even better one. You'll learn how to edit your own copy later. First, take a look at the reporter/copy editor relationship.

The Editing Team

A reporter and a copy editor working as a team will produce stronger and more readable stories than the two working separately. In this team-editing relationship, the reporter blends story familiarity and firsthand knowledge with the editor's experience, knowledge of structure and style, and outside observer viewpoint. As they work on a story together, the copy editor will learn more about the reporter's viewpoint of the story, and the reporter will learn more about the editor's viewpoint and the copyediting function.

To make the copyediting team concept work, both reporter and editor must adopt an "us" attitude. This means reporters must be prepared to accept the editor's suggestions for story changes, and the editor must allow reporters to question changes they don't think are necessary.

Furthermore, the copy editor should not revise or rewrite the story. That's the reporter's job. Copy editors should teach reporters how to edit and challenge them to become better writers. In this way, editors also become teachers of journalistic writing.

In learning to become a good copy editor, a reporter should be familiar with a stylebook. If your student publication doesn't have one, a model stylebook is included in the appendix. You should also learn the basic copyediting symbols, which are also presented in the appendix.

Content and Structure Come First

When you start editing your copy, don't begin by looking for style, grammatical, and spelling errors. Although correcting such errors is important, it's secondary to the overall purpose of the editing process, which is to produce the best story possible. For beginning copy editors, it may be necessary to go through a story four times. A story should be edited first for content, second for structure, third for grammar and spelling, and finally for style.

After practice and experience, the reporter/copy editor will probably be able to do a thorough job by going through the copy only twice. On first reading, the reporter/editor will check the story for content and structure, and on second reading, the emphasis will be on grammar, spelling, and style. But always go through a story at least twice. If a story has serious content and structure problems, it might be necessary to read through it several more times.

When editing copy the first time, the reporter/editor is looking for answers to several questions. The first questions should be, "Is this a complete story? Does it consist of facts that are important and give all of the necessary information to readers? Does it have lively quotes?"

After determining that there's enough content for a story, the next question is whether any vital information or necessary quotations are missing. A parallel question is, "Does the story leave any questions unanswered?"

Sometimes reporters will omit necessary information on the assumption that the reader "already knows it." This is where a copy editor with an objective and curious mind comes to the rescue. By asking questions a reader might ask, the copy editor helps the reporter add the additional information and quotes necessary for a complete story.

Another part of copyediting is eliminating wordiness. While checking for content, a reporter/editor should take out every word that isn't absolutely necessary and eliminate every quote that adds little or nothing to the story. The reporter/editor, through substitution and rearrangement of sentences, should find ways to say the same thing in fewer words and to change sentences from the passive to the active voice.

Assignment 1

On a separate sheet of paper, copyedit the following story for content and structure, remembering that spelling, grammar, and style are of secondary importance. Make notations for rewriting.

> Ten scholarships worth $1,000 each are going to be given to seniors at Wilston High School. Mr. Roy Vincent, principal of Wilston, said the scholarships are coming from four or five different companies.
>
> The scholarships have already been awarded to the seniors. One of the seniors who got a scholarship is Betty Armstrong. She said she's going to State University.
>
> Another scholarship is going to Robert Duncan, who is going to major in aerospace science. He's going out of state to college.
>
> Mrs. Winnie Snyder, the senior counselor, said Wilston High seniors have already been awarded an awful lot of

scholarship money and that it's probably a record of some kind.

Jesse Villareal, son of State Senator Victor Villareal, will get one of the scholarships, too. He wants to be an ambassador. He is also thinking about going into politics.

Alicia Chu will be getting a $10,000 scholarship for being named a Merit Scholar. She's the first one Wilston High has ever had. She's the valedictorian and has been in this country for only eight years.

Mrs. Snyder said Alicia is a really interesting person, and how she got to this country and Wilston High is really interesting.

Sara Applegate won a scholarship to Brian's Beauty College and is going to be a beautician.

Lewis Trammel got an appointment to the U.S. Naval Academy from U.S. Representative Jim Kissinger. Lewis was quarterback of the football team and was named the top quarterback in the state. He said he was real happy to be going to the Naval Academy.

Several other seniors got big scholarships, too.

Assignment 2

Copyedit the following sentences by removing unnecessary words. Use the copyediting symbols in the appendix. You may rewrite the sentence if you wish.

1. Johnston's Department Store has announced that it will again repeat its free offer of a free gift with each and every purchase totaling a sum of $5 or more, but that the offer will soon draw to a close.

2. An assembled crowd of people gathered during the month of July to celebrate Independence Day, the Fourth of July, in the city of Fort Williams.

3. After setting a new record in the 100-meter dash track event at the national track meet, he

returned back home to the place where he lived, for a period of two weeks during the summer months.

4. First of all, the future plans of the club call for all the newly elected members to be accepted and received into the organization during an initiation ceremony of induction.

5. The past historical records of the city during the year of 1986 definitely gave absolute proof that the dead body of a bald-headed man was found at the corner of Rogers and Seventh Streets, and it was positively identified by a red colored shirt as a personal friend of the mayor.

6. At the hour of noon, several invited guests from throughout the length and the breadth of the state came to a meeting held here during the course of the day to hear a talk on the subject of politics by the current incumbent governor.

7. When the game finally ended, the fightin' Tiger team here at Clarkston High had upheld all of the established traditions of the past and rewarded all those who were present in the entire audience with a victorious win over the opposing team, the lowly Bears from Frankville Tech, 7–6.

8. The principal of the school was given a report to the effect that several new recruits for the fall sport of football were brought together in a general meeting of everyone for the purpose of checking whether or not they would be eligible to play, and they will be eligible to play the game of football.

9. The man who wore a goatee on his chin and was indeed the proprietor of the antique establishment presented positive proof that the consensus of opinion was that it was an actual fact that the chair was a genuine old antique.

10. It was finally decided that the most complete way to prevent the breaking of an existing rule was to make a definite commitment to study all the different ways to uphold the laws currently on the books.

A Smooth Flow of Information

The next step to consider in copyediting is story structure. The main questions are these: Does the story read smoothly? Does the information flow from one paragraph to the next? Do the quotations add to and support the previous information? Are the facts and quotes presented in descending order of importance?

The copy editor must also consider whether a story would read better if certain facts or quotes were placed sooner or later in a story. Also, the editor must ask, are the paragraphs short, and does the sentence structure and length vary so that reader interest is maintained? If the story sounds choppy, transitions may be needed.

With a little experience, a copy editor can check a story for content and structure on the first reading. The second reading, then, is for checking grammar, spelling, and style. This is where a dictionary, a thesaurus, a stylebook, and a student-faculty directory come in handy. In addition to correcting errors, the reporter/editor must make sure tense and person are consistent. Newswriting is usually written in third person, past tense.

People mentioned in a story must be identified fully and accurately, and information and quotations must be attributed. Any editorial comment must be eliminated. The reporter/editor should constantly look for word substitutions—colorful words and specific details—that can give the story greater impact.

Finally, a good reporter/editor never asks someone else how to spell a word. That's what a dictionary is for. In school publications, many spelling errors occur because reporters assume someone else knows how to spell. It may take longer to look up a word, but it will be correct and, chances are, you'll remember how to spell that word when it comes up again.

An Editing Blueprint

When editing someone else's story, the copy editor must keep in mind that the writer, not the editor, should revise or rewrite the story. If only minor changes are required, however, the copy editor can make them. For major revisions, the copy editor should make extensive notes on the copy. It isn't enough to tell reporters to rewrite their stories. They need a detailed blueprint of what should be done.

Ideally, the copy editor and reporter should go through the story together, so each can ask questions of the other. Often, this isn't possible, so the next best method is for the copy editor to go through the story—at least twice—make notations, and then sit down with the reporter and go through the story.

Not only does this help the copy editor and reporter to work together as a team, but it gives each a better understanding of the other's role. It also gives the copy editor an opportunity to answer the reporter's questions and provide details about suggested revisions.

One final tip. When going through a story for the first time, read through it completely. There shouldn't be a mark on a piece of copy until it has been read once—start to finish. That's the way a reader is going to read the story, and that's the way the copy editor should read it too—from the reader's point of view.

Also, since there is a strong tendency to look for misspellings and style and grammatical errors, it's easy to get trapped into concentrating on these areas during the first reading, and to neglect content and structure. Remember, in the mechanics of copyediting, content and structure are the most important considerations. Grammar, spelling, and style are secondary.

Assignment 3

Copyedit the following stories for grammar, spelling, and style on a separate sheet of paper. Use the copyediting symbols you've learned and be very careful. Read through the stories before you begin editing.

A scholarship valued at worth $5,000 will be awarded to Brighton High School senior principle Sam winforth announced today. The scholarships made available by the brighton Boosters club will be given to the graduating senior who in opinion the of the boosters club scholarship awards board has excelled in academics extracurricular activities and in civic Work. "We had expected a two thousand dollar grant so the five thousand dollar scholarship is a pleasnt suprise, Wineforth said. interesting seniors can apply forthe scholarship by picking up a applacatin form in the councilors senior office.

After thirty yreas of teaching english and sponcering the CLASSICS Club at Berrydale high, mrss. roberta Stone will reteir to her lake cottige on Lkae Arrowpoint She says she will miss workin with studnets; but she wont miss

grtading all those appers. "ive had some very good studnets
but i've also had some studnets who gaveme fits, mrs stone
siad lloking bakc over the 30years though I wouldnt' chaneg
a day of ti'. the Bored of education planns to honer mrs.
stone at a special reseption whjch willbe held in the Room,
Board prior to theregular bi monthly meeeting on Mon.
December fifth.

Summary

An excellent news story can be improved through strong copyediting. Reporters should carefully edit their own stories before turning them over to a copy editor. Copy editors and reporters should then work together as a team to produce the best story possible. In the editing process, content and structure should be considered before grammar, spelling, and style. If rewriting is necessary, the editor should provide a detailed outline for the reporter to follow.

6 Out in the Field

The editor of a daily newspaper once said, "If I had to choose between hiring a good writer who is an excellent interviewer, and an excellent writer who is a good interviewer, I'd take the excellent interviewer. He or she will consistently come up with better stories."

Good interviewing and the research underlying it are absolutely essential for excellent reporting and writing. Together they form the first of the three **R**s of professional journalism: **Research, Report,** and **Rewrite.** Even press releases, churned out by corporate publicity departments, require background research to make them timely and relevant. Club meeting minutes, written by officers or sponsors, require considerable additional information before they are ready for publication. This material is gathered through interviewing.

At the junior high or high school level, the information for most news stories can be gathered with minimal research and interviewing. The information necessary for a two- or three-paragraph story reporting the results of a chess club match can be handled by asking two or three questions of a few people. But even a minor story requires some research and interviewing.

The Story Idea

Most beginning journalists assume that the first step in reporting is receiving a story assignment. However, the idea for the story must come before the story can be assigned. It's easy to draw up a list of events, past and present, add this to a roster of active clubs and organizations, and come up with a list of story assignments.

But top school publication staffs look beyond the usual "What's goin' on?" level of reporting. They want stories that have depth, high reader interest, and social relevance. These stories might tackle such subjects as the quality and cost of education, book censorship, teen alcohol and drug abuse, dating, teen stress, and career opportunities.

Where do these ideas come from? The sources are as varied as the ideas. One of the best sources is other school publications. Many school staffs exchange newspapers with other publication staffs in the area and state.

Wise staff members grab exchange papers as soon as they arrive and look for story ideas for their own newspaper. If your school newspaper exchanges with other schools, see what other staffs are reporting to their readers. Are there subjects that would be of interest to your readers?

Staff journalists should also read the local daily newspapers, scan weekly news magazines, and examine teen magazines for story ideas. In addition to reading for information and enjoyment, reporters read everything with a key question in mind: Is there something here we can use for a story in our newspaper? It could be the story itself, or it could be something in the story—a quote, a photograph, or even an advertisement—that could spark a story idea.

Assignment 1

Using the story guidelines discussed in this chapter, make a list of ten stories you would like to see published in your school newspaper. Share these ideas with the class. Then see if you can come up with ten new story ideas that weren't mentioned during the idea-sharing time.

Generating Story Ideas

The staffs of many top school newspapers devote at least one class period per issue to the development of story ideas. Each staff person is asked to bring several story ideas—usually five to ten—to class. The ideas are discussed; then a schedule of story assignments is drawn up for the next issue.

The purpose of class discussion is to help develop angles to the stories, determine what sources should be checked and interviewed, aid the reporters in preparing a list of questions to ask, and to set realistic deadlines that allow thorough development of the stories.

When drawing up a list of story ideas, five guidelines should be applied. First, and most important, the idea must relate to the readers' interests. This means that the potential story must either directly or indirectly affect the students.

This doesn't necessarily rule out stories that concern faculty or administration. Nonschool stories, such as the battle for teenage listeners by local radio stations, might also be developed into effective articles.

Second, the idea for a story must be practical. For example, it's virtually impossible to gain backstage access to a rock star for an interview. On the other hand, it is possible to talk with arena officials and develop a story on the preparations necessary for a successful concert.

Third, the story idea must focus on one specific angle. It's not enough to say, "Let's do a story on homecoming." Instead, you might suggest an interview with the homecoming queen from five years ago to see what effect the honor has had in her life. Or, you might suggest a story detailing the preparations necessary to stage a successful homecoming parade or dance.

Fourth, story ideas should avoid the obvious. School publication staffs should be aware enough to know that the major and minor sports along with major school events will be covered in the press. Assuming these stories will be covered, look for unusual sidelines and unique angles.

Fifth, carefully consider the traditional criteria for newsworthiness. Make sure that one or more of the elements—timeliness, proximity, consequence, prominence, drama, oddity, emotion—is present. Keep in mind that story ideas from out-of-state or national publications can be pertinent if you use local information and quotes.

Assignment 2   Take your three best story ideas and make a list of the people you would interview. Then make a list of at least five questions you would ask each person. Share and discuss your news sources and questions with the class. Help each other develop additional angles, news sources, and key questions.

Researching the Story

Once ideas are discussed and stories are assigned, reporters should learn as much as they can about the subject. Where or from whom did the story idea come? What are the possible angles to take? Who should be interviewed, and where can these people be found? What sources of additional background information are available? When is the deadline? These are the basic questions. Keep in mind that there are several potential sources for each story. For example, there could be three "layers" of sources for the Spanish club: The sponsor, club officers, and members. The depth of your story will determine the number of "layers" of sources you need to interview.

Utilizing this information and whatever additional research is necessary, reporters next draw up a list of key questions to ask the sources. With thorough background research, not only will reporters learn the answers to several important questions, but the questions they prepare will also be more meaningful, thereby resulting in better information.

Generally, three to five key questions should be prepared for each source. They should be questions the readers would like answered and questions that cannot be answered with a simple *yes* or *no*. In the case of a major interview or an in-depth story, the prepared list of questions should total twenty to twenty-five. There'll be plenty of additional questions to ask during the actual interview.

In most interview situations, whether it's the chess club sponsor or a U.S. Senator, the reporter should set up an appointment with the source. When making the appointment, either in person or by telephone, reporters should always identify themselves, tell whom they represent, and give the reason for the appointment.

When asking for an appointment, give the source a choice of times, based upon your most convenient times. Very likely the interview can be arranged for your convenience. In addition, a time-choice question can subtly move the source past thinking about being interviewed to trying to pick the best time for the interview. Also, have your questions ready and be prepared to conduct the interview when you set up the appointment, in case the source decides, "This is as good a time as any."

Assignment 3 Choose a major international, national, state, or local news story from a metropolitan newspaper. Make a list of questions you think were asked to get the information contained in the story. Share your story topic and questions with the class.

Assignment 4 Make a list of at least twenty people in your school who could be the major source of information for a news story for your school newspaper. Using the guidelines discussed in this chapter, determine the news stories for which they could be interviewed. Pick the three story ideas you like best; then make a list of at least three key questions to ask each source.

Conducting the Interview

When it's time for the interview, the reporter should make sure the questions are arranged so the easy-to-answer ones can be asked first. This helps place both the source and the reporter at ease and initiates a two-way conversation. Many reporters write their questions in a spiral-bound notebook, leaving several lines of space to record a source's answers.

A source's answers to questions will invariably prompt more questions, and the answers will reveal additional information. For this reason, it is sometimes better to work with a separate list of questions, as you'll have room in the notebook to record these additional answers.

Besides a list of questions and a spiral-bound notebook (one with the spiral at the top is easiest to handle), the reporter should have at least two pens or sharpened pencils on hand. Similar precautions should be taken if a tape recorder is used. Reporters should make sure they know how to operate the tape recorder, test it, and check the batteries.

If a tape recorder is used, permission for its use **must** be obtained from the source before recording begins. People who are unaccustomed to being interviewed by the media—especially in a school situation—are often intimidated by a tape recorder.

Taping without permission is inconsiderate and can bring an interview to an abrupt halt. Instead, ask the source for permission to record the interview in order to ensure accuracy. Although some people are uncomfortable with tape recorders, they will generally tolerate them if they know it's to ensure accurate quotations.

But a reporter should never rely entirely on a tape recorder. Batteries run down, recorders malfunction, tapes are often fuzzy and garbled. In addition, if a reporter uses a recorder without taking notes, hours will be wasted playing the tape several times over to obtain the information needed to write the story.

The purpose of a tape recorder for an interview is twofold: first, to ensure accuracy, and, second, to serve as a backup to the reporter's notes. A good reporter takes notes as if no tape recorder were being used.

Assignment 5 Assume that a well-known person is coming to your class to discuss an important topic or event. Draw up a list of questions you would ask this person. Share your questions with the class.

First Impressions

At interview time, punctuality is very important. Being late is rude and often puts the source in a bad frame of mind. This may cause the reporter to be flustered and ill-at-ease. When meeting the source, reporters should reintroduce themselves, name the publication represented, and restate the reason for the interview. After preliminary greetings, the reporter should move quickly to the first question and begin the dialogue.

For unprepared reporters, taking notes can be intimidating. The source starts rattling off a lot of important information, while the reporter is still trying to write down the first sentence. Most journalists who haven't learned shorthand develop their own method of speed writing to keep up with what the source is saying.

"Reporter's shorthand" generally consists of writing key words and leaving out small words like *the, a, an, and,* and *to.* In addition, experienced reporters abbreviate whenever possible. Only the reporter needs to be able to read the notes, so neatness doesn't matter as long as the notes are decipherable.

A good way to develop interviewing skills is to practice listening and writing at the same time. An enjoyable way to do this is by listening to your favorite music on the radio and writing down the lyrics of each song. Not only will you become proficient in taking notes, but you'll be able to sing along with most of the songs on the radio.

Another way to keep up with the source's comments is to throw in a relatively unimportant question; then catch up with your writing while the source is giving information you know you won't need. Also, don't be embarrassed by gaps of silence, and don't be afraid to ask the source to wait while you catch up with your note taking. By saying, "I want to make sure I get this right," you'll impress the source with your devotion to accuracy. However, if the source continually has to slow down while you catch up with note taking, you may lose the spontaneity of the interview.

With experience, a reporter learns what information to write down and what to omit. A good reporter will always ask more questions and write down more information than is necessary. It's always better to have more information and quotations than you need than to work with notes that don't answer all the questions.

Assignment 6

Invite a school administrator, local government official, or other potential news source to your class to discuss his or her work or another subject of interest to students. Make a list of at least five questions to ask this person. Take notes and then discuss with the class the information you think is significant.

Summary

Skillful interviewing is essential to strong writing. But prior to interviewing comes the process of finding story ideas, followed by thorough research. After the assignment of story ideas, the research provides a list of basic questions to ask interviewees. With such a list, reporters are prepared to conduct interviews on a professional level. Through careful listening, observation, and accurate note taking, reporters will have the material necessary to produce award-winning stories.

7 Featuring the News

ost journalists will tell you that they enjoy writing feature stories the most. Feature stories add interest and life to a publication. But even though they are fun to write, they are also difficult to write well. The fun part of writing feature stories is using your creativity. It is satisfying to know that you, the writer, have produced a written work of art that is there for all your readers to enjoy.

But because there's no limit to creativity in feature story ideas and writing style, it's sometimes difficult for a beginning writer to know where to find a story idea, what kind of information and quotes to get, and what writing style to use. Even experienced journalists often find it difficult to know where to begin and how to end a feature story.

Like a news story, a **feature story** begins with an idea and some possible angles. Next comes research, interviewing, and gathering information. After reviewing the information, the writer must decide what the story's special angle is, then determine the best way to play up or "feature" that particular angle. Outlining, writing, editing, and rewriting are the final steps.

Where do feature story ideas come from? The process is much the same as for news story ideas. In fact, a news story might be the source of several feature story ideas. One difference is that news stories generally depend upon a news event and timeliness; feature stories can appear anywhere, anytime, and don't have to be timely.

Brainstorming for Story Ideas

One of the best ways to find feature story ideas is to participate in a brainstorming session. Like writing a story, though, research must be done before the brainstorming session begins. The first step is to look for ideas in daily newspapers, exchange newspapers, magazines, books, and on television. Consider other people, their lives and interests, or even your own life and interests.

Many books and even more articles have been written on feature writing. Most of them list anywhere from five to twenty-five categories of feature stories. Here are a few that are common in school newspapers:

News feature. A news feature is a tory based upon a news event that has already been covered by the newspaper. Although a news story reports the facts of an event, there's often more to the story than just the facts. There's the story behind the story. For example, your school may have had a successful homecoming parade. The parade is news, but a feature story could explore why the parade was successful, using interviews with the students responsible for making it a success.

Interpretative feature. Similar to a news feature, the interpretative feature looks into the why or how of a news event. It analyzes the facts of a news story to explain the causes and motivations leading to the event, then discusses the possible consequences. Generally requiring a lot of research, the interpretative feature should provide the reader with a deeper understanding of the news event. An example would be an in-depth explanation of why the school board voted to eliminate off-campus lunch privileges.

Straight feature. This is a general category referring to any interesting story about a person, place, or event that has no "news peg" or timeliness associated with it. Straight features can range from observations on the beginning of spring, to a story about a football player in sewing class, to the frustrations of having to wear braces.

Personality feature. When a person wins an honor, accomplishes a significant goal, takes part in an important or unusual event, or possesses a unique hobby or talent, he or she can be the subject of an interesting feature story. In a personality feature, the writer's objective is to make the reader aware of the subject's personality by detailing the person's experiences, thoughts, mannerisms, and actions.

Interview feature. Similar to the personality feature, the interview feature is usually about a prominent individual or an authority on a particular subject or event. But the interview feature centers more on information obtained in an interview than on the subject's personality. However, the interview feature will have higher reader interest if the subject's personality is brought out in the story.

Human-interest feature. A "drama" story that appeals to the reader's emotions, the human-interest feature is always about a person or group of people. It can be humorous or sad, suspenseful or fast-paced. Human interest features establish a mood and provoke an emotional reaction in the reader. They are among the most popular stories in a newspaper, but they're also among the most difficult to write because it's easy for the writer's ego to get in the way. The writer must work on accurately reporting the drama involved in a story. It's harder to describe real emotions than to attempt manufacturing them, but it's the best way to write a human-interest story.

Brites. This is a newspaper term for brief, usually humorous, feature items. Brites are seldom more than 100 words long and focus on humorous things that happen in everyday life. The periodical best known for using brites is *Reader's Digest.* Unlike feature stories, brites have a definite pattern. They begin with a clever lead that grabs the reader's attention and go on to a brief, chronological description of an event that builds swiftly to a climax—usually a surprise ending—or to a catchy, summary thought.

There are other categories of feature stories, but these seven give you a good idea of the variety of feature stories you can write. Now that you know what kind of feature stories to look for, you can start generating story ideas.

Assignment 1

Using a metropolitan newspaper, preferably the Sunday edition, clip out three examples of feature stories for each of the seven categories listed in this chapter. Share them with the class, and briefly explain why you find them interesting or boring.

Personal Observations

Just as the success of an interview depends on the quality and quantity of research, the success of a brainstorming session depends on what the participants put into it, both in research and personal involvement. Although good story ideas can come from other publications and media sources, the best come from personal observation. This means you need to be vitally aware of your surroundings, the people around you, and the scope of their lives.

Most writers refer to this awareness as an intense curiosity. Reporter and feature writer Bill Ruehlmann, in his book *Stalking the Feature Story,* calls it acquiring the "camera eye." Reporters who want to be feature writers must approach every second of their lives as a picture to be captured and preserved in words for the reader.

Ruehlmann urges reporters to concentrate on what is going on around them. He points out that a reporter must see and understand things before he or she can communicate them. The writer must be both observer and participant. That is not easy. Seeing life through the camera's eye is like thinking—it takes dedicated practice to become good at it.

The beginning journalist especially must concentrate on looking for story ideas. A good way to start is to practice taking "mental snapshots" of your surroundings. Preserve the scene in your mind, analyze it, and then ask, "Is there anything here that could be turned into a feature story?" If there is, write the idea down. If not, erase the picture and take another.

At first ideas may be scarce, or they'll seem dull and uninteresting. That's okay. Make a list of ten to twenty story ideas, then keep the best five or ten.

After a time, you'll find you're observing more of life than ever before, and your list of ideas will grow in quality and length. That's the list you want to take into a brainstorming session.

Assignment 2   Using the news story ideas criteria found in Chapter 6, make a list of twenty-five feature stories that could be written for your school newspaper. Be prepared to share them with your class in a brainstorming session.

Assignment 3   Select your best five story ideas and then develop a list of possible sources and questions for each one. Discuss them with your class.

Conducting Brainstorming Sessions

Brainstorming sessions are most successful with small groups. From two to fifteen participants works well, though a group size of three to ten works best. Each member should bring a list of feature story ideas to the session.

After a secretary is appointed, each participant briefly describes one feature story idea, including the feature angle. (Refer to the guidelines for news story ideas described in Chapter 6 and use those criteria to determine story value.) Keep in mind that timeliness is now less important in judging a feature story idea.

At this point, there should be no discussion or criticism of the ideas, although it's permissible to ask questions to clarify the ideas presented. The secretary writes down each story idea. Participants should pay careful attention to the ideas offered, and if they think of another angle or a different approach, they should write it down for future discussion. They should also note any additional story ideas that come to mind and present them at the appropriate time.

After several rounds of idea presentations, and after the lists have been exhausted, participants can offer different angles to the ideas already presented. By this time, a long list of ideas is ready, and participants can begin focusing on the best ones. The stories can then be assigned to individual writers. The remainder of the list can serve as a backup for future assignments.

Now that story assignments have been made, the research begins. Several feature angles should be considered; informational sources need to be thought up, discussed, and listed. A list of questions needs to be written, and appointments made. Interviews should be conducted using the techniques described in Chapter 6. In feature writing special emphasis needs to be placed on capturing the subject's personality or the environment of the event.

Think in terms of "painting word pictures," then look for sights, sounds, actions, and gestures that can help a reader visualize exactly what a person or a scene looks like. In other words, be able to place the reader in the scene.

Assignment 4   Conduct a brainstorming session for feature ideas. If your class is large, you might want to divide into two or three groups. Each group should produce a list of its ten best feature story ideas to present to the class.

Bringing Out Personality

Before the interviews, be sure to have questions on your list that will help you get beyond the surface of your interviewees. Ask them, for example, what adjectives they would use to describe themselves. Then ask them to give examples of something they do that would typify each of those adjectives. You might also ask them what their happiest or saddest moments in life are, what their pet peeves are, what things they like best and dislike most about themselves, or what is the one thing they would change about themselves.

All of this information and descriptive material, along with many quotations, is necessary for the main focus of the story. This is the essence of reporting—serving as the readers' eyes and ears so that they can picture themselves as being there.

After you have the descriptive material, quotes, and essential information, it's time to review your notes, determine what angle will work best for presenting the story, then search for the most interesting facts to use in opening up that angle. Before you begin writing, however, keep in mind that the structure of a feature story is different from that of a news story. In Chapter 8 you will look at the techniques professional writers use to create the word images readers remember—those verbal portraits known as feature stories.

Assignment 5

Pair up with another member of your class. Conduct an extensive interview with your partner and also have your partner interview you. Get enough information to write a 200- to 300-word feature, interview story, or personality sketch about your partner.

Assignment 6

Write your name on a slip of paper and put it in a container with the names of others in your class. Draw names for a "secret partner." Without revealing the name you drew to anyone but your teacher, contact that person outside of class and arrange for an interview. Get enough information about your classmate so that you can present six interesting facts about the person or something he or she has done, without revealing the name. Tell the class the six facts you've learned, and then have them guess who the person is. Be fair to your classmates: Avoid using obscure facts, such as shoe size or a cousin's name.

Summary

Feature stories are an enjoyable form of writing for most reporters. But features can also be the most difficult to write because of the great variety of ideas and writing styles. There are many different kinds of feature stories, but as is the case with news stories, feature stories begin with ideas. Personal observations usually provide the best feature story ideas, and brainstorming sessions can help provide a large number of story possibilities. After stories have been assigned, interviews should be conducted to bring out the subject's individual personality. These personality traits and careful attention to other details will provide the information that brings a story to life.

8 Inside the Feature Story

Reporters can be great storytellers. In their jobs, they meet many people and observe many aspects of life. Their experiences provide them with fascinating material to keep listeners entertained for hours. The best reporters put this story-telling ability to work by writing feature stories.

A feature article is a good story told well. As one editor said, a news story is like a textbook, and a feature story is like a novel. To be well-rounded, you read both. You turn to the textbook for information and knowledge. You pick up the novel for entertainment and escape.

Just as the well-rounded reader reads both fiction and nonfiction, the versatile reporter must be able to write both news and feature stories. In some ways, writing a feature story is like writing a novel. Both a feature story and a novel need a compelling opening to capture the readers' attention. Both must involve readers in the plot, keep them interested, and move them quickly through the story. Both must conclude with an ending that ties up the loose strands and leaves readers satisfied and, perhaps, a little sorry that the story is over.

There is, however, a major difference between a novel and a feature story, and it is not length. A novel can be entirely fictional, but a feature story must be factual. Even though feature stories are based on facts, that doesn't mean they read like news stories. One of the problems with many feature stories in school newspapers is that they start out well but then rapidly deteriorate into rehashed news stories.

A different thinking process is required for writing a feature story. In a news story, the reporter concentrates on presenting facts in descending order of importance. In a feature story, the writer tells a story not only to inform but to entertain. Using novel-writing techniques to bring facts to life isn't as difficult as it sounds. You might think you know nothing about novel-writing style. Don't worry. You don't need to be a skilled writer, but you do need to be a good reporter.

Painting Word Pictures

A news story has two parts—a lead and a body. A feature story has three parts—a lead, a body, and a conclusion. The last paragraphs can be stripped from a news story, and a story still remains. But cut the ending of a feature story, and you leave nothing. The parts of a feature story in order of importance are the lead, the conclusion, and the body. A good way to write a feature story is to begin with the lead and then write the conclusion, before writing the body of the story.

The essential ingredient of a good feature story is extensive, thorough research. You also need many quotes and descriptions to put your reader into the word picture you're painting. A good reporter is observant and takes many notes. And, like painters, good reporters are on the scene to record accurately what they will paint in word pictures.

For an example, let's look at a professional at work. Reporter Steve Levin of the *Dallas Morning News* was assigned to interview a firefighter who had helped battle an apartment blaze that claimed five lives. Here are his first paragraphs:

> The smallest of the children wore diapers and pink pajamas, her hair in braids. They found her on her back on the double bed in the smoky haze of the bedroom. Her eyes were closed.
>
> Back at Fire Station No. 6, Capt. James Carlin held his hands two feet apart to show her size and then stared away, remembering the sight. The rubber band he'd been twisting in his hands went back to work, stretching and contracting, back and forth. Two other firefighters looked at the room's concrete walls. They all remembered the sight.
>
> And they all wanted to forget it.
>
> They had just returned from fighting a two-alarm apartment fire Wednesday morning at 2408 Meyers St. in which five small children died.
>
> Carlin sighed, the loudest sound besides the television in the kitchen.
>
> "When I saw the first one I picked him up and he wasn't breathing," he said quietly. "He was burned too bad to be alive. When I put him down, I saw another one inside the room and another one. Every time I picked one up, I could see another one. You could tell they were dead. I kept hoping the next one I found would show some spark of life.
>
> "I've never had to look five dead babies in the face before."

It was a tragic story for a reporter to cover, but Levin proves to be a master storyteller. Notice that he does more than simply interview the firefighter. He starts immediately with a description of one of the victims and then switches to a description of Carlin playing with a rubber band. That's good observation and note taking.

Notice also how Levin observes and reports not only the sights but the sounds and even the mood of the fire-station room. Through his observations, notes, and storytelling talents, Levin takes his readers into the room with him, where they hear the firefighter's story in his own words. In addition to being in the fire station with Levin interviewing the firefighter, the reader is also in the burned-out apartment with Carlin, experiencing his feelings as he finds the victims, one by one.

Writing a Better Foreign Student Story

Here is another example, this time taken from a school newspaper and a typical story assignment—interviewing a foreign student. Like professional reporter Steve Levin, reporter Diana Moore of Spring Woods (Texas) High School goes beyond the usual interview story.

> The classroom is filled with soft giggles and murmurs as everyone discusses who they went out with last night, the latest concert, or the outcome of the Oiler-Steeler game.
>
> Although she sits in the center of everything, one girl is not part of any conversation. Instead, she sits alone with no one to talk to. She has just come to Houston from Korea. Her parents speak no English and, for most of her life, she has lived in a way most Americans cannot begin to understand. She has lived in a country that demands strict discipline and obedience. She has lived through war and changes in government and has seen her country torn apart. Now, she faces a different culture, government, and people.
>
> But most frightening of all for students like sophomore Ok Kim is the loneliness of the language barrier.
>
> "It's very hard . . . no one will speak to me," she said.

Moore could have written an interview story, filled with quotes from Ok Kim, and it would have been a good feature story. However, by vividly describing the scene, Moore makes the reader aware of Kim's language and social barriers. In addition to producing an excellent story, Moore's work had another result. After the story was published in the school newspaper, many students adopted Kim and her family to help speed their learning of the English language and American customs.

In the stories by Levin and Moore, the readers not only learn what is taking place but feel the emotions of the people involved. That's good journalism. It is also good reporting and feature writing. An outstanding feature writer always looks for ways to turn an ordinary story into a memorable one by involving the reader on an emotional level.

Assignment 1

If a school administrator, local government official, or other news source addressed your class, as suggested in the Chapter 6 Assignments, use your notes to write a 200- to 300-word feature story about the speaker's presentation.

Assignment 2 Use your notes from the classmate interview suggested in the Chapter 7 Assignments to write a 200- to 300-word personality sketch about your interview partner. Feel free to conduct another interview, if necessary.

Adding Details

You can enhance the appeal of a feature story by adding details and descriptions that pull the reader into the story. Here are a couple of leads from feature stories as they might appear in school newspapers, followed by the leads Houston, Texas, high-school journalists actually used in their publications.

> The Spanish club sold piñatas for Christmas this year to help the needy in the community. They raised $3,000, which bought four poverty-level families food for a month and Christmas presents for the fifteen children in the four families.

A better lead:

> Tears ran this courses down the face of the thirty-year-old mother of five. The pile of toys—including a basketball, a red wagon, and a soft-bodied doll—lay in a heap in the middle of the cluttered little living room. Behind it, on the table, sat boxes of canned goods, spaghetti and beans, and a frozen turkey.
>
> This was, according to Virginia Smith, the first real Christmas her babies have ever had—and the first one she could remember in over a decade.
>
> The sale of 500 piñatas made this scene possible in four homes, Spanish club member Joanna Rodriquez explained.
>
> "I think we could have sold more if club members could all go see this stuff being delivered. I even cried when I told my mother about it," Rodriquez said.

Here's another lead,

> Math teacher Stark Mallow is good. In fact, he's so good that he was named teacher of the year for the state of Texas.

A better lead,

> His hand swept over the board, big sweeping motions obliterating thirty minutes' worth of work as students scrambled to jot down the last figures before they disappeared.
>
> "I've never seen anybody work so fast and furiously. He's like a computer spitting out information. I've never seen anyone so smart," Jennifer Barlow said of math teacher Stark Mallow.
>
> While his knowledge and quickness may have seemed computer-like, his way with students was not.
>
> "I wasn't surprised he was named math teacher of the year for Texas. It's hard to believe I get so much from just an hour in class," calculus student Clyde Simpson said.

Mallow spit out another problem, chalk clacking as punctuation to the remarks he made as he wrote.

"He makes learning fun. He manages to show us everyday applications and joke us through our mistakes until we understand," Barlow said.

<table>
<tr><td>Assignment 3</td><td>Using one of your best feature story ideas, sources, and question lists developed in the Chapter 7 Assignments, conduct an interview and write a story that could be used in your school newspaper.</td></tr>
</table>

Catchy Leads

By now it should be obvious that the lead sets the tone for the feature story, and the descriptions and specific details transform it into a verbal work of art. There are many ways to begin a feature story. Let's look at ten of them.

The **descriptive lead** is detailed and vivid. It should paint a clear and precise picture of a scene, an individual, or an event and set a mood for the reader. It should enable readers to visualize exactly what is taking place.

> The four o'clock bell blares throughout the building, followed by the trample of students' feet pounding down the halls. Soon, all is quiet and the dust begins to settle, but just for a moment. It isn't long before the dust, paper wads, candy wrappers, broken pencils, and other trash are whisked away into a dustpan with the swish of a broom guided by an experienced hand.
>
> The students' day is over, but for custodian Irma Miller and other janitors, it will be awhile before they start home.

The **narrative lead** is similar to the descriptive lead. But whereas the descriptive lead describes a scene, the narrative lead tells a story. Though it is also descriptive, the narrative lead is more like a play with a scene, characters, and dialogue.

> "What are you students doing out of class?"
> Holding a white mug with Anderson Orchestra and his name boldly emblazoned in blue, new principal Ron Beauford lowered a practiced gaze upon a dozen students moving down the hall toward the counselor's office. The question bore a semblance of threat, a touch of incredulity, as if Beauford could not believe the insolence of these youngsters. His tone also left no doubt that he expected an answer.

The **summary lead** is used for an in-depth or news-oriented story. It tells the reader immediately what the story is about, then goes into detail, using quotations and description to complete the story.

> Standing in line at a snack bar, the average student orders a cheeseburger, a cold drink, and a bag of chips. Eating his lunch, he

or she doesn't think about the content of texturized vegetable protein in the cheeseburger, the percentage of sugar in the cold drink, or the amount of preservatives in the chips.

The school district reserves that job for the district food services department, which, in addition to handling the nutritional concerns and feeding 21,500 students a day, also deals with federal budget cuts and the elimination of several federal programs.

The **contrast** or **comparison lead** points out the opposites or similarities in a situation to familiarize the reader with its uniqueness.

His wealth is reported at $200 million. He controls a handful of corporations, operating in more than twenty nations. Yet he carries his lunch to work in a brown paper bag and wears the latest fashions from Sears and Roebuck's bargain basement.

Or,

Rice, squirtguns, newspapers, and confetti are all a definite yes. A definite no is to admit it's your first time there. If you do, you'll have a minimum of five people pointing at you and yelling "virgin" as the slide projector-spotlight focuses on you. In Houston, this advice is to be followed at midnight in the Alabama Theater at *The Rocky Horror Picture Show*.

The **shocking statement lead** usually consists of a short, snappy sentence in a paragraph by itself, with additional details following in the second paragraph. It's designed to get the reader into the story before revealing what the story is about.

It's the ultimate computer game.
The rewards: satisfaction, fun, and prestige among peers. The penalty: a possible felony conviction. Just the high stakes game for those weary of the usual fare found in arcades. It's called hacking, and it consists of breaking into the computer records of banks, schools, and even highly sensitive governmental agencies, either for fun, to alter records, or to steal information or services.

The **suspense** or **teaser lead** is similar to the shocking statement lead. It involves the reader by building suspense before revealing the focus of the story.

Alone.
There's a sound upstairs. The first stair creaks. A second step follows.
"Who's there?"
Silence.
Bodies become tense, eyes close in expectation. The music builds. All wait. Then comes the scream. . . .
There is something between the buttered popcorn and the fear of walking through the dark parking lot to reach a car that makes people love to watch horror films.

The **literary** or **historical allusion lead** uses a parody on a literary or historical phrase or refers to a familiar scene or character. This type of lead should be used only when the parody or reference is appropriate or natural, as in the following examples.

> Caesar came, saw, and conquered. The Spartans came, saw, but left bruised, battered, and bloodied in defeat.

Or,

> Winning isn't everything . . . it's the only thing.
> That was the philosophy Coach Vince Lombardi followed all his life. And it was the philosophy he expected his players to follow as well.

The **direct address lead** refers to the reader as *you* and addresses the reader as though in a dialogue. This lead works especially well when the writer uses descriptive language with which readers can identify, as shown in this example:

> Now then, parents, the important thing is to stay calm and remember you were once young, too. Be happy if your kids listen to you when you speak, do their homework every day, help around the house, and come home when they should. If you can claim to be so lucky, should you really be worrying about the kind of "haircut" your kid is sporting?

The **quote lead** begins with an exact quotation, but it should be used only when what is said is so striking that it compels the reader to go further into the story.

Although it's an easy way to begin a story, most quotes are not dynamic enough to pull a reader in. The following quote lead does work:

> "Don't be mad. I took some pills," Karen Keaton cried as she stooped over the toilet.
> A few hours later, the fourteen-year-old freshman died after a series of cardiac arrests. . . . One by one, she had swallowed each of the 250 heart pills taken from her mother's recently refilled bottle.

Like the quote lead, the **question lead** is often misused in school journalism. It should be used only when the question relates directly to the feature angle and compels the reader to seek the answer further in the story. Unfortunately, most question leads can be answered with another question: Who cares? Here's an effective question lead.

> How can you watch people die and not have it affect you?
> It's a question paramedic Ron Shandlin is asked all the time, but never has an easy answer for.
> "I usually tell them I think more about the people whose lives we save," Shandlin said. "But you can't just make the memory of the others go away. It stays with you."

In Conclusion

Just as a feature story can be opened in many ways, there are also several ways to conclude it. The **lead replay,** or **summary ending,** for example, is commonly used and refers back to the feature angle presented in the lead. Here's the ending to the Christmas charity story used earlier in this chapter.

> Christmas morning was really special in Virginia Smith's home. Her two-year-old Patty played mommy with her new doll named Sara. Her three-year-old packed the trash in his wagon and pretended to haul it to the dump. Her fourteen-year-old hooted in the drive as he sunk another from his imaginary free-throw line. And Virginia smiled at the scene as the smell of turkey roasting permeated the air.
>
> It would not be a Christmas soon forgotten.

The **proximity ending** is also a common conclusion and uses information from the preceding paragraph to provide the angle for the closing. Often a quote is used as in the case of the firefighter story.

> "We've made the same [type] run hundreds of times," Harris said. "We were just concerned with getting dressed so that we'd be ready when we got there. When it's a call with people trapped inside, it pumps you up. And then we get there and all these kids are dead."
>
> "You try to forget about things like this," Ramirez said. "You have to, or it will drive you crazy."

The **restatement ending** reminds the reader of the feature story's purpose by restating it. In the example of the school food-service feature, a restatement ending might read like this:

> It's not an easy task. The district food services department must prepare a budget beset by federal cuts and elimination of programs. Yet its main purpose is to plan and provide nutritional meals for 180 days, at a reasonable cost, for 21,500 students with finicky taste buds.
>
> It makes choosing between a cheeseburger and a Sloppy Joe look like a piece of cake.

The **word play ending** uses a play on words, alliteration, or a catchy phrase to close feature stories and leave a lasting impression in the reader's mind. However, care must be taken not to overdo using these techniques. In a feature story about the efforts of Future Farmers of America (FFA) members to ready their hogs for an upcoming district competition, the effective ending reads this way:

> So, while members of the aerobics class are dancing and kicking their way to slimness and health, FFA contestants are busy grooming and feeding their animals for success in the judging ring. And while the aerobics students are convinced thin is in, the FFA is equally convinced fat is where it's at.

Another common way to close a feature story is with a **quote ending.** As with the quote lead, however, the quote ending must be striking and memorable. The story about the girl who died after taking her mother's heart pills started and ended with a quotation:

> Since the death of their oldest daughter, the Keatons have found themselves becoming more protective.
> "I find myself watching for things," Mrs. Keaton said. "I'm not sure of what. I'm just watching."

One of the most effective endings for a feature story is the **surprise ending.** The writer builds suspense in the story, then startles the reader at the conclusion. Care must be taken not to drag out the story or make the surprise obvious before the end. In a Florida high school yearbook story, Marianne Savalli recounts an interview with a fourteen-year-old cancer patient who was fighting to lead the normal life of a high school freshman.

> "I've always said I'm going to write a book someday and that it's going to be about me," Cheryl said. "I've read all those cancer books: *Eric* and *Sunshine,* but they left me in tears because the person dies. This book would be different because I'm still alive—and intend to stay that way!"
> On March 1, Cheryl died in her sleep at Shauds Teaching Hospital, Gainesville.

Assignment 4

From your local newspaper, find and bring to class examples of the different types of feature story leads and endings presented in this chapter. Discuss whether they are effective.

Assignment 5

You are a reporter for the Williamston High School *Bugle.* From the following information, write a 200- to 300-word feature story for your newspaper's first issue of the school year. You may use any statements attributed to individuals as direct quotes, or you may paraphrase them, but you may not change the meaning. Leave out unnecessary details.

The Situation

Jeff Hagan is a fourteen-year-old freshman at Williamston High School. He is the younger brother of Scott Hagan, a senior at Williamston. Jeff is a member of the Key Club, Student Council, and National Forensic Society. He is also a member of the cross country and tennis teams.

The Hagans live at 2328 Hillside Drive. During the summer, Scott Hagan fell through a glass storm door at the family's home. Jeff was at home at the time, but his parents, Mr. and Mrs. Frank Hagan, were at work. Mr. Hagan is an insurance salesman. Mrs. Hagan is an obstetrical nurse.

Quotations

Jeff Hagan. I was watching television when I heard this crash. I ran downstairs and there was Scott, bleeding all over the place. I almost panicked, but realized I was the only one at home. I remembered what they say in Boy Scouts—that if the face is pale, elevate the tail. And that's what I tried to do.

I knew I had to get him to the hospital immediately. I propped him between the bucket seats of our car, his head on the back seat and his feet up on the dashboard. I had watched Dad drive, and twice last spring I started the car and drove a few feet in the driveway. I got the keys out of Scott's pocket. There was blood all over both of us. Scott wasn't screaming. He just said, "It sure hurts."

The car has an automatic drive. I couldn't have made it if I had to shift. I drove mostly with one hand, keeping the other on Scott's cut chest to try to keep the blood from running. At times, I hit sixty miles per hour. I didn't have time to think it over. I just went.

Everything moved so quickly. I don't remember the drive to the hospital at all. After they took Scott into surgery, a nurse walked me to an office. Mom and Dad were there. Then, I really started to cry. I couldn't stop for a long time.

Frank Hagan: Scott's chest was ripped open to the rib cage by jagged glass, and the nerves, tendons, and artery in the right armpit were severed. He'll need two or three years to regain the use of his right arm. They give him a fifty percent chance he can use it.

He has a lot of interest in flying. He wants to be a corporate pilot, and he's logged thirty hours' flying time. I know his interest in flying will be a big incentive as he tries to regain use of his arm.

Jeff has never driven a car in his life. How he got Scott in the car and made it to the hospital is a mystery.

Mrs. Frank Hagan: I was on duty when they brought Scott in. I asked Jeff, "Who called the ambulance?" He said no one. He drove. I couldn't believe it. I saw Scott in the recovery room after surgery. He looked up at me and said, "You know, Mom, that Jeff is one cool kid."

Dr. Norman Garrett: I was preparing for another operation when Scott arrived. He was in such bad shape that I had to move right to him. But it could have been so much worse. Because his brother brought him in so quickly, we still had time to work on him. If there had been a delay, he could have arrived dead. There had been a tremendous loss of blood.

Extra Information: The trip from the Hagan home to the hospital is just over five miles. The accident took place at 11:45 A.M., and Jeff was forced to contend with heavy noon-hour traffic. Jeff is 5'2" and weighs 120 pounds; Scott is 6'1" and weighs 190.

Putting the Magic 3 to Work

The information a reporter gathers determines what kind of lead and ending works best. After deciding the feature angle, try three different lead approaches and pick the one that best grabs the reader's attention and captures the mood of the story. After selecting the best lead, write three different endings and pick the one that best fits the story.

Then begin writing. The feature theme should be well developed, with facts presented in logical sequence. Include interesting quotes and smooth transitions. People should be identified fully and accurately, and the writing should be concise, vivid, and precise. Avoid slang and clichés.

After editing, the feature should be rewritten, edited again, then shown to a friend or co-worker for an honest appraisal. Ideally, the feature should be rewritten a second time before being submitted for publication.

If you think feature writing is a lot of work, you're right. The quality of a feature story depends on the amount of effort you put into reporting and writing. But the admiration of your peers and the satisfaction you gain from writing a good feature story makes it worth the effort. In addition, you'll be surprised at how much fun you'll have doing the writing.

Assignment 6

You are a reporter for the Williamston High School *Bugle*. From the following information, write a 150- to 200-word feature story for the next issue of your school newspaper. You may use direct or indirect quotes. You may not make up facts, but you do have the freedom to develop the setting as you think it might have been.

The Situation:

Williamston High School is located in the suburb of a city with a population of approximately 500,000 people. The school enrollment is 2,600. Many of the students are sons and daughters of State University faculty and staff or of employees of four major computer manufacturing firms.

Susan Sanchez is the school counselor. She is thirty-four years old and a graduate of the University of Michigan. She is married to Dr. Roberto Sanchez, a professor of chemical engineering at State University. They have two children, Bianca, 10, and Doug, 6.

Ms. Sanchez has implemented a program to assist overweight students in coping with the stigma of obesity. She has worked closely with Dr. Danita Washington, a psychologist, and nutritionist Debra Matsumoto. The program consists of counseling, diet, and exercise.

Quotations

Susan Sanchez:

With everyone involved in fitness, from a psychological standpoint, a child who carries around a few extra pounds has more of a dilemma now. There's a stigma in this society to being overweight, and kids pick up on it. They watch television and see that all the heroes are slim, and the villains are often obese.

It is important to realize that no kid wants to be fat. The *New England Journal of Medicine* recently produced the first concrete evidence that genetic influences play a deciding role in the weight of adults, ranging from marked thinness to fatness. It's not an environmental thing. It's not a lack of self-discipline. Overweight kids tend to be ridiculed, taunted, and ostracized. They hear nicknames like Fatso, Jelly-Belly, and Tubby. Unless the child is very strong, this can be devastating to his or her self-esteem. What we're trying to do in this program is to show these children that they can control how they feel about themselves and the rest of the world.

Dr. Danita Washington: Like adults, children want to lose weight for various reasons. Although most children don't understand the health benefits of attaining and maintaining a normal weight, they know the social reasons too well. Obese children complain of being teased or stared at. A lot of the girls say, "I'll be able to wear pretty clothes, and maybe boys will pay more attention to me if I lose weight."

Debra Matsumoto: There are no miracle cures. You can't sleep away those pounds, regardless of what you hear on television. The new cure for fatness is no miracle at all; it's simply good nutrition and exercise.

We want the kids to change their lifestyles. First, they have to be committed to losing weight. Then, we try to see what psychological reasons might lie behind the weight problem and to make sure there is adequate family support to sustain the child through what could be a life-long weight control program.

Then, the child begins a ten-week program of diet, counseling, and exercise.

Jeffrey Beaumont, sophomore: I weigh about twice what I should. I've been fat all my life. Not just overweight, but really fat. This program has really helped me. Before, when someone teased me about my weight, I'd console myself by eating. I'd look for satisfaction in food, generally sweets.

I've tried all sorts of diets, but they never worked. This time, I'm really serious. I'm running every day. I'm watching my diet, and in about six weeks I've lost thirty pounds. I have a long way to go, but I have a picture in my mind of how I want to look, and I'm not giving up until what I see in the mirror matches the picture in my mind.

Summary

Writing feature stories is like writing novels. Both rely on a strong opening to gain the readers' attention, a fast-paced story to keep them involved, and a conclusive ending that leaves them feeling satisfied. The best feature writers paint word pictures of sights, sounds, and moods to pull readers into the story, maintain their interest, and help them visualize the situation. Leads and conclusions are vital to feature stories. Leads set the tone, and conclusions tie the story together. Top professionals write several leads and conclusions for their feature stories, select the best ones, then write their stories. After writing, they carefully edit, add more details and description, then rewrite their stories before submitting them again for publication.

9 Editorials—That's Your Opinion

If news stories are the flesh and bones of a newspaper and feature stories are the spirit, then editorials are the brains. A student newspaper can inform and entertain, but if it doesn't influence its readers by providing analysis and persuasion, then the publication can be considered mindless.

One of the essential roles of a newspaper is to provide editorial leadership for its readers. In the school community, a major part of the newspaper's responsibility is to serve as an open forum for student comment and concern. Without fulfilling that leadership role, a student newspaper becomes nothing more than a school bulletin or public relations newsletter.

Administrators are sometimes afraid to allow student journalists free expression because they believe students will be irresponsible in handling this freedom. Unfortunately, this has sometimes proved true. But such cases are rare and are far outweighed by the mature, thoughtful editorial leadership practiced by school newspaper staffs throughout the nation.

The ingredients for editorial leadership in a school publication are a comprehensive editorial policy (discussed in Chapter 2), a willingness to consult with school faculty and administrators on issues that might be considered sensitive, and a commitment to demonstrating responsibility in opinion writing.

Editorial Variety

The first step in achieving editorial responsibility is to recognize that the purpose of student editorial pages is not to continually criticize school policy or personnel. Criticism is only one of several forms an editorial can take. In fact, there's more to the sophisticated opinion page than editorials. Excellent student editorial pages also contain cartoons, perhaps a student-drawn comic strip, current student opinion, music and movie reviews, news analysis, guest columns, and letters to the editor.

In addition to this variety of features, there are various types of editorials. The responsible staff makes sure its readers are offered that variety throughout the school year. Editorials are persuasive—never pompous or preachy. They deal with local people and situations, such as the local reaction to national and international issues. They don't have bylines—they represent the opinion of the newspaper staff as a whole. Like other classifications of writing, editorials can be categorized many ways, including the following eight types.

Persuasive Editorial

Perhaps the most common type of editorial in student newspapers is the **persuasive editorial.** This type attempts to sway the reader to a particular point of view. It can support or oppose a current viewpoint or action, and then recommend a course of action.

Structurally, the persuasive editorial explains the proposal, action, or viewpoint in question, takes a stand, lists and explains reasons for taking this stand, then closes with arguments why the reader should agree with the stand. An example would be an editorial urging the administration to honor academic achievement by awarding academic letter jackets to students in the top ten percent of each class.

Explanatory Editorial

Another familiar editorial is the **explanatory editorial.** This kind of editorial is usually tied to a news event, an action recently taken, or a proposed action. Although the main purpose of the editorial is to explain the causes of an event or recent action or the reasons behind a proposed action, it also takes in the possible effects of the situation. In many instances, the editorial will support what has or what will happen, or it may call for further study of the situation.

The explanatory editorial describes the event, action, or proposal, then explains the causes and reasons involved. This is followed by an assessment of importance, a look at possible effects, then a statement of support or a call for further study. An example of an explanatory editorial is one that explains the causes, then supports an administrative decision to switch homecoming activities to another weekend so they wouldn't conflict with the celebration of Rosh Hashanah.

Critical Editorial

The **critical editorial** is also common in high school publications and, unfortunately, is easily abused. The best critical editorials use a reasonable tone, logical thinking, and offer solutions, suggestions, or alternatives. The weak ones, on the other hand, are irrational, harsh, poorly researched, and offer no solutions or alternatives. They are nothing more than gripe sessions in print.

A critical editorial begins with a brief explanation of a problem and states the need for change. A discussion of weaknesses, errors, or causes follows. Then a solution, suggestion, or alternative is offered, along with supportive reasons for the proposed action. A typical critical editorial might disagree with a school policy of suspending students for conduct violations and suggest instead an in-school suspension policy that features a secluded room and a study monitor.

Laudatory Editorial

Seldom seen in any but the best school newspapers is the **laudatory editorial.** Members of a school community often do commendable deeds, yet receive little or no recognition. In addition, nearly eighty percent of the comments people receive in life consists of criticism. A laudatory editorial simply praises or thanks an individual or group for accomplishments or actions.

The structure of a laudatory editorial consists of identifying the group or individual to be praised and describing the achievement accomplished. After an explanation of why commendation is deserved, the editorial concludes with a brief statement of praise or thanks. This type of editorial can be written when an individual or group wins a contest, does something that benefits the student body, or brings recognition to the school and community.

Editorial Commentary

The **editorial commentary** usually takes the form of an editor's column or a column by another staff member. However, the commentary can represent the staff's opinion and be unsigned (printed without a byline) and presented in the same fashion as any other editorial.

The editorial commentary makes an observation or comments on a situation. Its purpose is to provoke thought about, or perhaps encourage, participation in the situation. Subjects for editorial commentary might range from the value of spring break, to the celebration of spring itself, from the joys of being a senior, to a critical appraisal of new fashions.

Leadership Editorial

The finest school newspapers do more than editorialize on current situations. They plan editorial campaigns to bring about change in their school environments. This requires the **leadership editorial,** usually presented in a series. This type of editorial seeks to initiate programs, actions, new policies, or changes in attitudes or direction.

The first of the series defines the goals, explains the reasons for attempting these goals, and outlines the steps necessary to achieve them. The closing paragraph urges readers to support efforts to attain the goals. Additional editorials target intermediate goals, present periodic progress reports, and comment on the status of the campaign. Topics for leadership editorials might be to eliminate censorship of library books and classroom literature, a drive to clean up the campus or prevent vandalism of school property, or a push to form a student advisory council to meet periodically with school board members.

Entertainment Editorial

Entertainment editorials, like editorial commentary, usually appear as columns. On occasion, however, a student newspaper staff might run an entertainment editorial in the form of a typical editorial. Not to be confused with music or movie reviews, entertainment editorials have a serious point to make but do so in a light, usually humorous, fashion.

By using anecdotes, exaggeration, satire, or other forms of humor, the writer identifies and comments on a current situation, with the point coming at the conclusion of the commentary. At no time, though, should the humor be vengeful or directed against individuals or groups or their personal beliefs. An example of an entertainment editorial would be a list of suggestions, ranging from renting guard dogs to hiring local artists to cope with the graffiti problem in school restrooms. The purpose of the editorial, of course, would be to point out the need for a solution to the graffiti problem.

Mini-Editorial

Finally, there is the **mini-editorial,** or **mini-torial.** This is an expression of opinion that can be stated in one, two, or three paragraphs. Mini-torials have a specific point to make and many times offer a solution to a problem. A mini-torial, for example, could point out the need to clean up and polish trophies in a display case, then recommend that a student organization take on the task as a project.

Assignment 1
From issues of a daily newspaper, clip one example of each of the eight editorial categories described in this chapter. Share them with the class; briefly describe their structure; and then explain why you find them convincing or not.

Assignment 2
Using the news story ideas criteria found in Chapter 6, make a list of fifteen editorial ideas that could be written for your high-school newspaper. The angle should include a recommended stand and a suggestion for the type of editorial that could best present the idea. Be prepared to share your ideas with the class in a brainstorming session.

Writing Effective Editorials

Most student editorials are explanatory, persuasive, or critical. Now look at what it takes to write these editorials well. The necessary steps are similar to those for writing interesting feature stories. Find a worthy topic, determine the stand to be taken, and then do research to support the proposed stand.

In-depth research is very important before writing editorials. Beginning writers are sometimes hesitant about writing editorials because they're afraid readers will criticize their opinions or think they're of little value. Research can help allay those fears. In addition to writing an editorial with valid reasoning, the writer will be able to effectively answer most arguments against the stand.

A good way to research and write editorials is to approach the task as though you were an attorney preparing for a trial or a debator preparing for a debate.

Not only must you gather information to support your side of the case, but you should anticipate arguments against your case, then find counter-arguments to refute them. Once you have information on both sides, discuss it with a knowledgeable friend. Determine the two or three best arguments favoring your stand, the strongest arguments against your stand, and then the best counter-arguments. Now you're ready to write.

Begin the editorial with a concise explanation of the problem you're addressing, then state the stand you're taking. List and explain, if necessary, the two or three reasons you're taking this stand.

Next list and refute the major arguments against your stand. If necessary, present a solution or recommendation for the situation. And, finally, restate the editorial objective with a call for action. There are other ways to construct an editorial, of course, but for the beginner, this trial-attorney or debate approach is an effective structure that can be varied according to circumstances, your imagination, and your writing abilities.

Assignment 3	Select your five best editorial ideas. Then develop a resource list for researching them. Discuss these with the class.

Assignment 4	As a class, brainstorm for editorial ideas. Break into smaller groups if you have a large class.

Elegant Editorializing

In rating the persuasiveness of student editorials, experienced judges look for several factors. The lead of an editorial should grab the reader's attention and present the issue, as well as present a definite stand.

The language should be simple and uncomplicated, and the overall wording and editorial tone should be positive. In addition, the presentation should be clear, logical, reasonable, and fair, avoiding exaggeration.

An editorial must deal with principles and ideas, not with people and personalities, and should offer the reader direction in thinking, action, or both. It should not be preachy or have a superior attitude, nor should it criticize or belittle anyone's ideas.

Editorials are written in first-person plural (*we, us, our*) and are always localized, timely, and related specifically to your readers. They should run between 150 and 200 words, and rarely, if ever, longer than 300 words. As a final note, judges point out that the best student editorials offer original solutions for problems.

Like feature stories, well-written editorials take time and effort, but it's especially rewarding when other students agree with your opinion. It can be even more exciting when people act on your recommendations, or when actions benefiting the student body are accomplished as a result of your editorial. That's when you realize you've plugged into the power of the press.

Assignment 5	Use one of your best editorial ideas, do the necessary research, then write an editorial that could appear in your school newspaper.

Assignment 6   You are an editorial writer for the Millwood Valley High School *Echo*. Based on the situation, write a 150- to 200-word editorial for the next issue of your school newspaper. You may support or criticize any action taken; you can offer suggestions or recommendations for change or call for whatever action you think necessary. Choose any style but keep in mind the nature of your audience and the function of the editorial.

Situation   A mandatory assembly for juniors and seniors was held at 9:30 A.M., Tuesday, in the Millwood Valley High School auditorium. The assembly began with Principal J.T. Parish introducing Warren Clark of the National Citizens for Good Music Committee. Clark was accompanied by Rev. Arthur Timpkins and Mrs. Madolyn Daniels. All three reside in Stanton, Virginia. Clark is a former business executive, and Daniels is the wife of U.S. Representative Charles Daniels. Timpkins is pastor of the largest church in Stanton.

Clark, Timpkins, and Daniels presented a strongly antirock music program. The program included brochures, a slide presentation, and an emotional discourse on the religious implications of the music issue. Only the antirock music point of view was discussed. The assembly lasted an hour and forty-five minutes. Halfway through the assembly, two senior girls, Debbie Loggins and Rhonda Smith, walked out. Neither spoke as they rose from their seats and left the auditorium. The assembly continued without interruption. That afternoon, both girls were called into the principal's office and suspended from school for the remainder of the week.

Pros   Students are expected to remain in their seats during a mandatory assembly, unless they are confronted with a medical emergency. By walking out, the girls embarrassed the school in the presence of invited guests. The campaign against rock music is an issue that generates strong emotions, but the administration thinks students need information upon which to base their opinions and emotions.

Cons   The school does not have the right to delve into issues of personal taste, such as rock music. If these issues are to be discussed, both sides should be presented, and emotional rhetoric should be avoided.

Quotations

Principal J.T. Parish: The action of these two girls created a substantial disruption of the assembly. It's true they left the auditorium quietly, but their action swayed the attention of the remainder of the students away from the presenters to the action of these two girls. It was an embarrassment to the school and to the rest of the students who remained in their seats.

I do think the punishment fits the crime. The school has a specific policy dealing with mandatory assemblies, which states that students must attend for the duration of the program except for medical emergencies. I am not allowing my personal opinions on the rock music issue to interfere with my duties as chief executive of this school. The policy was broken. I assume Debbie and Rhonda opted to suffer the consequences for violating the policy.

Debbie Loggins: In the first place, the assembly should never have been presented. It wasn't educational. It was propaganda. My parents don't pay taxes so that I'm subjected to one person's side of a controversial issue. I think they were trying to brainwash some of the kids. And then, when they started playing on our religious beliefs, that's when I decided I'd had enough.

I can't believe they suspended us for three days. I'm going to miss two major exams, and it's going to hurt my grades. I've been an honor student all four years, and this could ruin my chances for a college scholarship. I just can't believe this is all happening.

Rhonda Smith: My parents are outraged. They're talking to an attorney. maybe they could get away with this kind of thing back in the 1950s, but they can't today. If someone had walked out of a mandatory assembly featuring Bozo the Clown, nobody would have blinked an eye. But for this, they try to destroy our high-school careers.

Lisa Wellington, junior: This program was informative, to an extent, though I'd rather have heard both sides. When Debbie and Rhonda walked out, I didn't think a lot about it. It certainly didn't embarrass me, and it didn't seem to embarrass the people around me.

Additional Information No lawsuit has been filed, although Larry Smith, Rhonda's father, said he would request that both girls be allowed to make up lost class time. If denied, he said he will file suit in the State District Court.

School Board Member Leona Robertson said she will ask that a committee be formed to establish guidelines for selection of mandatory assembly topics. "If we're going to provide assemblies on controversial topics, both sides must be presented," she said.

Summary

Editorials are the brains of a newspaper; they are the *think* pieces. Contrary to popular belief, editorials aren't necessarily critical. A variety of items are found on the editorial pages of today's school newspaper with opinions expressed in many different features. Editorials are designed to persuade, not to anger. The most effective persuasive editorials begin with in-depth research on both sides of an issue. Then the facts are presented in much the same way an attorney argues a case before a jury. Effective editorials deal with issues rather than personalities. When written well, editorials can change minds and help solve problems.

10 Sports and Entertainment— Fun Writing

How? Why? These are the two most important questions in journalism, particularly in specialized writing, such as sports or entertainment. How did the Fightin' Turtles manage to sneak up on the Runnin' Rabbits and win the game? Why did Coach Thunderpuss pull his star forward with four minutes left in the game? How does Sylvester Starstruck's new film compare to his last? Why did the Screamin' BeJeeBees decide to produce a CD of romantic ballads?

When student journalists begin asking more "how" and "why" questions, coupled with a sense of timeliness, they'll stop writing about subjects their readers already know or don't care about.

Take sports for example. In many school newspapers, sports coverage consists of column after column of play-by-play accounts of games that are two weeks, or perhaps even two months, old. And for sports features, readers usually get the Athlete of the Month, a shallow interview story that, at best, reveals that Wanda Wonderstuff's favorite meal is peanut butter and jelly.

When these same readers turn to the entertainment page, they're greeted with reviews revealing the storyline of movies that have been showing for a month. Or they're faced with a review, filled with gushy generalities, of a reporter's personal experiences at the Screamin' BeJeeBees concert six weeks ago. Or they're subjected to a review of a three-month-old CD, consisting primarily of information about the lead singer, lifted from a month-old copy of a supermarket tabloid.

Most people like to read about athletes and entertainers. Unfortunately, school sports and entertainment reporting is often dull and flat. You can change this by learning to ask more "how" and "why" questions, by looking for different ways of presenting information, and by demanding timeliness in sports and entertainment writing.

Better Sports Reporting

Better sports writing will follow when better reporting takes place. Many school sports writers don't attend the games they're supposed to be covering. Those who do attend do so as spectators, becoming involved in the emotion of the game, and don't bother to take notes. After all, they can get the results from the local paper, obtain a quote or two from the coach, and their job is done—or so they think!

A much better approach is to report sports events just as you would report news events. First, make sure you understand the sport you're covering; then make sure you understand the assignment by discussing it with the staff. Next comes research. Make a list of interview sources and questions to ask. Obviously, your primary sources will be the coach and key players.

Questions should deal with the significance of the event (game, meet, or tournament), who's favored, which players or participants should be watched, the relative weaknesses and strengths of the opponents, offensive and defensive strategies, and each team's game plan.

In addition to acquiring this advance information, it would be helpful to attend a few of the team's workouts. Learn what's involved in getting ready for a swim meet. Get a feel for the relationship between a cross country coach and the participants. Learn the importance of taping and deep-heat therapy.

Not many outsiders attend practice sessions of local school teams until they reach the championships. So, if you're willing to spend time getting to know coaches and participants on their home turf, they'll recognize your efforts and very likely be more cooperative and open with you. And you'll have an advantage when these teams make the championships.

Assignment 1

Prepare to cover a sports event at the varsity, junior varsity, B-team, or freshman level. Prepare a list of questions and sources. Discuss your list of questions and sources with the class.

Gathering Material

Whether you realize it or not, you now have enough material for a major sports story. Combine what you hear and learn during practice sessions with your advance information, and you'll have the material for an excellent preseason or **preevent story.** Also, you'll have good background information for the upcoming game, as well as for future sports features.

When it's time to cover individual events, you'll already know which participants to watch on each team as well as what plays to look for during the event. This means you'll be busy taking notes, depending on the pace of the event. Track or swimming, for example, are easier sports to cover than basketball or hockey.

It's important to keep track of scoring, assists, and other individual performances, but it's equally important to note exciting moments and turning points. In addition, at the end of each period, jot down a few words to sum up what's happened so far and what the outlook is for the next period. If you have time, speculate on why things happened the way they did, and then predict what will happen next.

At the end of the game, swing into the next phase of reporting. Summarize the notes you've taken, and highlight the points you want to clarify or emphasize. Remember, you're looking for story angles, along with answers to the "how" and "why" questions that came to mind during the event. Next talk to players or participants, coaches, and perhaps officials, if necessary, to get quotations and answers to your questions. Again, you'll want more quotes and information than you think you'll need.

After your postgame interviews, go through your notes to pick out your story angle. In most instances, the angle will evolve from one of the "how" or "why" questions. Rarely will your lead consist solely of the end results. Rather, it's more likely to center upon a turning point, significant performance, or an individual event that can be directly linked to the results.

In your story, you need to explain why your particular angle is important. You also need to discuss the event's significance and effect on the teams or individuals involved and describe and analyze the key moments of the event. Use direct quotes, when possible, to describe and support these story elements.

Assignment 2	Cover the sports event you've selected. Begin by interviewing your sources and gathering pregame information. Discuss your information with the class before attending the event.

Comprehensive Sports Coverage

If you're covering a sport for your school's biweekly or monthly publication, there won't be time or space to carry a comprehensive story for each game, meet, or match. This is especially true if you're covering basketball, since there may be two or more games a week.

This means you'll need to pick the most significant game, meet, or match and concentrate on developing a "how" or "why" angle for that particular event. It can be the most recent or the earliest. Just make sure it's the most significant. The other games can then be summarized in the story in two or three paragraphs.

Another system practiced by some of the nation's leading school sports writers is to highlight in the lead a team's upcoming event, complete with quotes from opposing coaches and participants. You can follow the same information-gathering criteria you would use prior to covering an event, and you'll have what's known as an **advance story.** Past events can be summed up in the body of the advance story and, if space permits, significant trends or an analysis of key moments can be included.

When the season is over, treat it like one big sports event. Gather your notes from the season, look for significant trends, draw up a list of questions, and then call on the coach and players. This time, you'll be seeking an analysis of the past season and the outlook for next year. But avoid the cliché, "Next year, we'll win 'em all." With this information, you'll be able to write a **postseason wrapup,** and you'll also have the basic information for several sports features.

Sports features should be treated just as you would handle feature stories on the news side. Brainstorm for ideas, develop several angles, make a research and source list, and then go after the interviews. One of the best aids in learning to write sports features is to read the sports section of metropolitan newspapers, sports magazines, and the sports pages of school newspapers. Note the story ideas and angles. Study the word choice and story structure of articles you like. Store them in a mental file and then adapt them for your stories when appropriate.

<table>
<tr><td>Assignment 3</td><td>Using the information you gathered prior to the sports event, combined with event and postevent information, write a story for publication in your newspaper.</td></tr>
</table>

That's Entertainment

Although most sports writing deals with news and features, entertainment writing consists more of features and opinion. Many school entertainment writers do a poor job because they don't know how to report well. As for excellent sports reporting, comprehensive entertainment reporting requires hard work and extensive research.

One of the basic differences between sports and entertainment reporting is that in sports you have access to coaches and players. In entertainment, the artists, directors, and producers are rarely available to student reporters.

In many school newspapers, entertainment reporting consists primarily of movie and music reviews. However, the best student newspapers include not only music and movie reviews but also reviews of books, plays, television series and specials, and videotape movies, as well as concert and ticket information, personality interviews, radio station comparisons, and commentary on local bands.

Readers who haven't seen a particular motion picture, or who haven't heard several songs from a certain CD, want to know one thing: Is this movie or CD worth what I'll have to pay to see or hear it? At the same time, people who've already seen the movie or purchased the CD want to know if the experts like it as much as they do. So how does one become an expert reviewer or critic?

Although it's not essential, a musical background is of great help in becoming a music critic, just as a film background is beneficial to becoming a movie critic. But what a student critic lacks in musical or film expertise can be compensated for through research.

From the reader's viewpoint, the quality that gives a critic expertise or influence is credibility. It's easy to have an opinion and state it in print. What's difficult is backing up that opinion with logical reasoning. If you write a review without research, your opinion will have no depth, no credibility, and no influence. Such a review is a waste of time for both you and your readers.

Backstage and Background

Before attempting to review a movie or a CD, research the performers involved. For a movie, learn something about the leading actors and actresses, as well as the supporting actors and actresses. Learn something about the director and the script writer. What have they done in the past? What is their background?

Have you seen any of their previous work? If not, use a VCR and videos and start viewing. How can you evaluate their performances if you have no previous material for comparison?

The same principle holds true for CD reviews. Learn something about the artist or group, the backup group and instrumentalists, the songwriters, the producer, their background, and their work. Compare this effort with their previous works.

In addition to researching movie and music principals, it's a good idea to research comparable movies and music by contemporaries. How does the style and ability of Tom Hanks compare and contrast with Steve Martin? How would you compare the directing of Oliver Stone with Spike Lee? Is Natalie Merchant better on her own or with 10,000 Maniacs? Is Oasis the Beatles of the mid-90s? If you can discuss such questions clearly in print, then you're on your way to becoming a critic.

Besides researching the performers and their contemporaries, check the industries and the professional critics. Find recent copies of *Billboard, Spin,* and *Rolling Stone* for music and *Variety* for movies. But stay away from the fan magazines, as they are often a waste of time.

To help learn the language and structure of comprehensive reviews, read *Time* and *Newsweek* for movie reviews and *Rolling Stone* for CD reviews. Also, check out the entertainment section of your local newspaper. Avoid doing a rehash of local reviews because your readers will recognize this immediately. Besides, those reviews are aimed at an adult audience, while you're trying to influence your peers.

Assignment 4	Clip out five movie or CD reviews from *Time, Newsweek,* or *Rolling Stone* and bring them to class. Discuss with the class what you think are the strengths and weaknesses of each review.
Assignment 5	Using these same reviews, rewrite them in language you think your classmates would better understand and appreciate.
Assignment 6	Using the same magazines or a local newspaper, clip out a minimum of five reviews of films you've seen, CDs you've heard, or both. Rewrite them and change the parts with which you disagree.

Researching to Overcome Fear

If you've never written a review before, it can seem threatening. The greatest fear you need to overcome is thinking you don't know enough. The best way to conquer that fear is simply to do your research, make a list of questions that you, as a critic, would like answered, watch the movie or listen to the CD, take notes, and then start writing your review.

Some questions you might want to address in a CD review include: How well are the instruments used and played? Do the lyrics have meaning? Is there a story line, and is there a lot of meaningless repetition? Is the vocal quality appropriate, and does it have feeling? Does the production distract from or overwhelm the music and lyrics with gadgetry and background sounds? Are the music and lyrics so weak that a lot of background sounds are needed to compensate?

When writing film reviews, there are several questions you'll want to address: Does the film move along? A movie's pace has nothing to do with action and violence. A film is either dynamic or static; it either keeps your interest or bores you. Is the film able to communicate a message without relying heavily on dialogue or emotional cheap shots? Are the scenes realistic? Do the characters act like real people? Is the dialogue realistic? Does the film appeal to your age group? Are there gaps in the dialogue or from one scene to the next? Is the film original, or have you seen similar scenes and heard similar dialogue many times before?

Remember, the basic question the reader wants you to answer is whether the film or CD is worth the money. So begin your review with a statement that indicates your overall opinion and answers this basic question. Next give a brief synopsis of the film's story line or the songs on the CD. But don't reveal the funniest moments of a movie or relate the entire story line, and never give away surprise endings.

Next give reasons why you like or dislike the film or CD, and then back up these reasons with examples. Don't be too one-sided, however. You'll see very few films or hear few CDs that have no positive qualities, just as in your student years, you'll probably not hear the ultimate CD nor see the greatest motion picture of all time. Therefore, you need to discuss strengths and weaknesses—the memorable and forgettable instances—and give specific examples.

Close your review with a summary of your reaction to the movie or CD, and then recommend some action to the reader, such as, "don't miss the movie" or "forget the CD and listen to the radio"—whatever you honestly think the reader should do.

By following this procedure, you'll soon become a knowledgeable writer about movies and music. And not only will your readers look forward to your reviews, but they'll also be eager to discuss their views and opinions with you— a recognized, respected expert.

Assignment 7

Make a list of the five best films you've ever seen and the five best CDs you've ever heard. Write down what you like and dislike about each of them. Present your list to the class, and be prepared to defend your choices.

Assignment 8

Review and research a movie or a CD of your choice. After viewing or listening, write your review as though you were writing for the school newspaper. Present your review to the class and see how many of your classmates agree or disagree with you.

Summary

How and *why* are the basic questions to ask and answer when writing sports and entertainment stories. Better sports and entertainment writing comes as a result of better reporting. Understanding the sport and its terminology is essential. Thorough research is required, followed by attendance at the sporting event. Interviews should follow the event and should give reporters valuable information that can result in several related stories.

Entertainment reporting differs from sports reporting in that it involves more opinion writing. Many of the principal participants won't be available for interviews. But, as for sports writing, research is essential for entertainment writing. Writing reviews can be intimidating, but research can help overcome that fear.

11 Getting a Head in Journalism

Teens and Crime
Students caught in the act tell their stories

Locked doors cause students to be tardy

A+ *Teachers helping students* Make the grade

"Intramurals gives me a chance
to play in sports I normally couldn't. . . ."
Jocks of all kinds

For Rachel Pollack, prom night was as bad
Only in her wildest dreams

You win some, you lose some
Football team loses district championship in last quarter

Band wins
Group beats 1400 other musicians
for Contraband's first place title

Student becomes movie star!

That caught your attention, didn't it? That's one of the two purposes of a headline—to grab the reader's attention. The other purpose is just as important—to tell the reader what the story is about. For many readers, headlines are like newspapers, something that appears out of the blue, something that is there every day. But, like newspapers, someone has to write headlines. To write them well takes almost as much work as writing the stories themselves.

Many student journalists consider writing headlines an undesirable chore. Some think headline writing ranks with folding and distributing newspapers and getting ink all over their hands and clothes. Maybe it's because of the severe space demands of headlines. A headline can't be too long or too short; like Goldilocks' porridge, it has to be just right. Or perhaps it's because of having to learn a method for counting the letters in a headline. And there are many other rules to learn when writing headlines.

Not only are headlines one of the most important parts of a newspaper, but writing them can also be one of the most creatively challenging jobs on the staff. In the process of producing school newspapers, headline writing is usually one of the last tasks undertaken. They are often written under the intense pressure of a deadline, and often with the attitude of "who cares what it says, as long as it'll fit." Several newspapers have taken much of the deadline pressure out of writing headlines by requiring them to be written *before* the story is written. Then, in the final stages of production, the headlines are modified, if necessary, to fit.

Headlines are a vital part of a newspaper because they're one of the first things readers see when they pick up a newspaper. They are like story leads except that they have fewer words and appear in larger type. If readers come across a dull or confusing headline, they'll very likely skip the story. Imagine how you'd feel if it was a story you'd worked on for hours to keep the reader interested, and it appeared under a dull headline.

That's why it's wise to learn to write headlines yourself. Then, if the need arises, you can write an attention-getting, clever headline for your own story—like putting the whipped cream and chopped nuts on your sundae. Better yet, you could become the chief headline writer for your school newspaper. Many staffs recognize that headline-writing is not one of their strengths, and when they find skilled headline writers, they put them to work immediately.

Headline writing isn't as difficult as most people think. The same student journalists who can write outstanding feature stories might chew their pencils in half when writing headlines. Admittedly, it can be frustrating at first, but once you catch on, writing headlines can become as interesting as crafting an exciting lead for a feature story.

The 'Tell-a-Friend' Method

There's a system for writing headlines that's so successful that it's used by most professional publications. It's called the **telegram** or **tell-a-friend** system. Here's how it works:

Read the story entirely before attempting to write a headline. As you read through it, write down the main parts of the story. One- or two-word phrases are all you need. Basically, you want to describe what the story is about, and that could include activities, names, and events. Next, check your key phrases and summarize the story in one complete sentence, as though you were going to tell a friend.

The story, for example, might consist of interviews with students who have moved out of their parents' homes for various reasons and are living on their own. Your summary sentence might be, "Several students say that while living on your own isn't as good as it sounds, it beats putting up with all the troubles at home." That's much too long for a headline, but you'll be able to condense it into one.

Since every word in a telegram costs money, you want to tell your friend what's going on in as few words as possible. Concentrate on using key words only, cutting out all the articles, *a, an, the,* and conjunctions, *and* and *or,* and other nonessential words.

Your sentence might then read: "Living on your own isn't easy, but beats home problems, students say." Notice how twenty-five words were condensed into twelve words. Also notice how you can change the sentence around and substitute words to make the sentence more concise.

Cutting the sentence in half is good, but let's see if you can do even better, while making sure the reader, or your friend, will still know what the story is about. How about, "Living on your own isn't easy, students say." You've left out the "home problems" part, but the condensed sentence still tells the reader what the story is about, and you're down to eight words.

Now you have a short sentence that can be turned into a two-line headline. "Living on your own" is the first line, and "isn't easy, students say" is the second line. Not a great headline, perhaps, but it's workable and fulfills the two main purposes of headlines: to get the readers' attention and to tell them what the story is about.

Writing Headlines

Once you've learned the tell-a-friend system of gathering basic headline information, there are several other guidelines to follow. But don't try to learn all of them at once. Study this section, start writing headlines, then check your headlines against these guidelines to see if they're written correctly. In time, you won't have to refer to the book.

The first technique is to make your headline simple and straightforward and to avoid the obvious. "More students cause increase in enrollment" is like saying, "More water causes rivers to rise." Don't give information in the headline that isn't in the story, and don't base the idea of your headline on facts buried deep within the story. If that's where the basic story information is, then the story may need rewriting. Your headline facts will usually come from the lead paragraphs.

The second technique for writing headlines is to use specific facts and avoid generalizations. "Swim team works hard" is weak. "Speed stressed during workouts" is better. When choosing the facts for your headlines, remember to limit them. Too many can be confusing. Also, avoid using label headlines. "Tennis results" is a label head; "Netters win/first match" isn't.

A third technique is to make a complete statement with each headline. Every head should have a subject and a verb, either stated or strongly implied. Headlines have more impact if you use the present or present progressive tense to describe past events, and the future tense to describe future events. Also, active verbs are more effective than passive ones. "Game won by team" is poor. "Trojans nip Owls" is better.

It is also important to match the tone of the headline with the tone of the story. A serious news story deserves a serious headline, and a light feature story can take a clever, playful head. However, be aware that while cleverness is okay, you should never sacrifice accuracy for wit.

Another headline technique involves choosing just the right words. Avoid repeating key words in the headline, or in a main headline and a secondary headline. Also avoid using forms of the verb *be,* such as *is, are, was,* and *were.* An exception to this rule is the infinitive *to be,* which can be used to describe a coming event. "Homecoming to be postponed" is an example. Finally, jargon—such as "grapplers," "tankers," and "tracksters" in sports headlines—and strange synonyms—such as "confab" for conference or "fish" for freshman—are pitfalls to avoid. Abbreviations and initials (except obvious ones, like FBI or NCAA, the school name, or a team name) also should be avoided.

The remaining techniques for writing effective headlines have to do with format. They include:

1. Don't use periods, and use commas in place of the conjunctions *and* and *or.* If two separate thoughts are expressed, separate them with a semi-

colon. "Students travel by car, bus to state playoffs," and "Play auditions scheduled; 17-member cast sought" are examples.

2. Use single, rather than double quotation marks.

3. Don't hyphenate words from one line to the next.

4. Avoid splitting verb phrases and prepositional phrases between lines of a headline, and don't end headlines with participles. Also avoid splitting ideas and names between lines. "Hopkinsville Fire/Department praised" is a bad split. "State honors/fire fighters" is better.

One final word of caution: Use alliteration very carefully (Proud Patriots pound pesky Panthers). Once per 100 headlines is too much!

Counting Units to Fit Space

Now comes the math part of writing headlines. Unless you are familiar with computers and use desktop publishing software, such as Adobe PageMaker or Quark XPress, this part will involve counting letters, numbers, punctuation, and even spaces between words to make sure the headline you write will fit the space allowed for it. With desktop publishing, headline sizes can be manipulated to fit the allotted space, and specific counting isn't usually necessary. However, journalists who use desktop publishing and know how to count headlines can generally write better headlines faster.

Suppose your staff doesn't use desktop publishing and your editor asks you to write a headline for a story. She says she needs a two-line, 48-point, four-column head with a 24-point kicker. Sound confusing? It really isn't. Take her request step-by-step.

First, there's the matter of **points.** The size of type is measured in points. Seventy-two points equal an inch. The type you are reading now is 11 points. Typically, headlines range in size from 18 points to 60 points.

Columns are the next consideration. The headline goes at the top of a story, and a story may run a single column or as many as six.

A kicker is a special kind of headline, most often a label like "Latest Election Results." It is set in smaller type above the headline and usually underscored.

To see what 48- and 24-point lines of type look like, you should consult your newspaper's headline schedule. This is a chart from which you'll learn that a 48-point, two-column headline can have a maximum of 14 units of space per line. A 24-point line of type, running a single column, also has a maximum of 14 units. Fine. but what is a unit? This, too, is not really complicated.

On most typewriters, all of the letters and symbols are the same size. This is not true, however, for type set by a typesetter. In this kind of type, the letter *M* is nearly twice as wide as the letter *I,* and the letter *t* is only half as wide as the letter *a.* To find out whether your headline will fit a given space, you have to allow for these different widths. The following chart is based on the unit count system. What it does is to assign values for all the characters set in type and for the spaces between words.

Unit Values	½	1	1½	2
Letters	j, i, l, t, f	most lower-case letters	m, w most capital letters	M, W
Numerals	1	most numerals		
Punctuation	most marks of punctuation	question mark double quotes parentheses	dash	
Spaces	spaces between words			

The 14 units of space for the headline your editor asked you to write are the limits your headline must adhere to. If your headline runs longer, you must find shorter words or drop words that aren't essential.

Confusing? Not really. Hard to do? Perhaps at first. But once you've written a few headlines, it becomes easier. If you're working with a computer, it becomes even simpler. You type your headline, and it appears on the screen. Then you tap a key that commands the computer to measure the headline. If it's too long, the extra letters may show up in a different color or be dropped to a lower line. Either way, you know you have to work on it.

However you write your headlines—with a computer, or with a typewriter, or by hand—you'll find yourself toying with the structure and rewriting. You'll substitute new words, especially verbs, looking for new ways to attract the readers' attention. That's when you start to have fun—creating headlines that make a lasting impression.

Assignment 1

Clip out ten headlines of two lines or more from your local newspaper. Bring them to class and put them in a container with the headlines brought in by your classmates. Next draw ten headlines from the container. Copy the headlines on a sheet of paper and number them from 1 to 10; then count the units in each headline and write the count for each.

Assignment 2

Exchange your ten headline counts with a classmate's. Count each other's headlines and put your count next to your classmate's.

Examples of typefaces that can be used for headlines

This is Baskerville regular, **bold,** *italic, bold italic*

This is Frutiger 55 regular, **bold,** *italic,* ***bold italic***

This is GillSans regular, **bold,** *italic,* ***bold italic***

This is GillSans Condensed regular, **bold,** *italic, bold italic*

This is Goudy regular, bold, *italic, bold italic*

This is Helvetica regular, **bold,** *italic,* ***bold italic***

This is Korinna regular, **bold,** *italic, bold italic*

This is Palatino regular, **bold,** *italic, bold italic*

This is Times Roman regular, **bold,** *italic, bold italic*

This is Utopia Headline regular, **bold,** *italic,* ***bold italic***

Assignment 3   Count out the following headlines; then tell what's wrong with each one, if anything.

Choir performed
Christmas concert

Students with a date
invited to the fall prom

Sophomores view films.
Freshmen are left out.

Ignorant answers destructive
to finding problem's solution

Cast, crew elated after winning state one-act play contest

More players means
a bigger football team

You should attend
classes regularly

Girls' track hindered
by inexperience, depth

Sophomores, juniors, and seniors
are going to the senior prom and dance

Students are stressed
by final exam schedule

Cold weather caused
by low temperatures

Homecoming is going
to be postponed again

Lectures, childhood stories
typical of student teachers

When job layoffs occur, the first to be fired are the students

Hockey game
final results

Smith's margin of victory
was 120 votes

Council president says
charity effort is "great"

Sr. has problem
with work sked

Chess club wins
chess tournament

LHS CC team
captures meet

Government class
attend council meeting

Baseball team
practices daily

Unusual movies provide interesting alternative to normal video fare

Visitors flock to Math
Department for fair

Fantastic victory
over the Bulldogs!

New attendance system
installed this year

Typing club plans
plans first banquet

Assignment 4

Write headlines for the following stories. The counts are given for each story.

1. *Write a three-line, one-column headline; each line should count not less than 15 and not more than 18:*

   Baby Bear broke down on the witness stand, and the golden-haired defendant pleaded that she was just seeking refuge from a storm.

   But a "federal" jury agreed that it was naughty of Goldilocks to rip off the Three Bears, and convicted her Friday of misdemeanor, petty theft, and malicious mischief.

   Her sentence: Serving porridge to Baby Bear for a month.

   Judge Eckhart Robinson, normally a federal bankruptcy court judge, led a jury of 12 boys and girls from Middville Elementary School in a lesson about criminal justice. The case mimicked real courtroom action, from jury selection to a dejected 10-year-old prosecutor, who thought the little girl got off easy.

   "The jury sympathized with her plight, but could not condone her actions," Judge Robinson said. "Since she is a first-time offender, we feel justice would not be served by a harsher sentence."

2. *Write a one-line, three-column primary headline, with a one-line secondary headline, which will run below the primary headline. The primary*

headline should count not less than 20 and not more than 24, while the secondary headline should count not less than 40 and not more than 44:

Outstanding extracurricular activities seldom help students with mediocre grades win admission to selective colleges, a Princeton University English professor told Middville students Monday.

Dr. William Webster said a recent study challenges the idea that colleges, in choosing their freshman class members, pay close attention to what students achieve outside the classroom as well as in it.

"First and foremost, colleges and universities are concentrating on grades," he said. "Extracurricular activities are fun and enriching, but your first priority must be your regular classwork."

3. *Write a one-line, four-column headline that counts not less than 33 and not more than 36:*

Middville's major and minor crime rates declined drastically from a period beginning last May until December, according to a federal government survey released Monday.

"We are very happy with the findings of this survey," Police Chief Gerald Minnow said. He credited the decrease to a new set of curfews aimed specifically at high school students.

"Our theory was that if we keep more people off the street after midnight, less harm can come to them, and we can devote more of our time to the surveillance of safety in and around the city," he said.

Chief Minnow stressed the importance of "preventing potential crime" as opposed to solving crime that has already taken place.

"Only when we have the staff and time to protect the city and prevent crime can we cut down the number of major and minor crimes," he said. Minnow added that the midnight curfew for persons 17 years of age and younger will be continued.

4. *Write a two-line, two-column headline, with a one-line kicker—a headline that will appear in smaller type above the primary headline. The primary headline should count not less than 16 and not more than 19, and the kicker should count not less than 16 and not more than 20:*

"The School Board has appropriated $55,000 for improvements to the school library," board president Marcus Whitman said Friday.

"The building renovation and resource improvement has been the number-one priority of the school board budget committee," Whitman said.

"We realize the importance of a full-service resource center, and the present facility is not serving that need," he said.

Ten percent of the allocation will be used for new carpeting, enlargement, and the addition of an audiovisual teaching aide facility. The remaining 90 percent will be spent toward updating reading material and revamping audiovisual equipment.

New reference books, including dictionaries, atlases, encyclopedias, digests, and reader's guides have already been ordered.

"We're not wasting time," Whitman said. "The renovation will begin in a week, and we hope to have the project completed by September 1."

5. *Write a two-line, two-column headline, with each line counting not less than 15 and not more than 18:*

"When I stepped off the bus and through the gate, that's the closest one can come to hell on earth. From me to you, crime doesn't pay."

This was the message 19-year-old State Department of Corrections inmate Darnell Rogers stressed to Middville High students Friday, during the school's annual "Operation Kick-It" assembly.

The assembly is part of a three- to five-inmate panel that travels around the state telling their stories in hopes of educating, informing, and warning high-school students of the results of drug abuse.

Rogers said he dabbled with marijuana in high school but eventually became involved in harder drugs.

"I soon became uninterested in school and started skipping classes," he said. "I couldn't get a job, but I needed money, so I turned to crime. Next thing I know, I'm sitting in a wire cage in the state prison."

Assignment 5

From a recent issue of your student newspaper, find five headlines you think are weak. Cut out the headlines and the stories and write new headlines for each story. Share them with your class.

Summary

Headlines have two purposes: to attract the readers' attention and to tell them what the story is about. Although there are many guidelines for writing interesting, clever headlines, the tell-a-friend system seems to work consistently. A unit chart and a headline schedule can help you make sure that headlines fit the allotted space.

12 Putting the Package Together

ewspapers, like the stories and headlines you write, don't just happen. You already know the steps needed to produce copy, but what does it take to produce the school newspaper itself?

An organization, a staff, and a plan are essential for producing a newspaper. Most newspaper staffs have an editor or coeditors and a middle management—page editors, section editors, copy and managing editors—advertising and photo editors, and production managers, anyone who directs other people and their work. In addition, there are reporters and photographers. These people are responsible for publishing the newspaper on a regular basis, which could be weekly to once every six weeks.

To publish a newspaper regularly, the editors and staff must establish and follow a production schedule. From initial story ideas, the schedule takes the newspaper through information gathering, writing, editing, rewriting, keyboarding or typesetting copy, proofing, advertising sales, and page composition and printout or pasteup, to printing, sales, and distribution.

To better understand this procedure, assume that you and your classmates are going to organize a school newspaper. You've called a meeting, and everyone is there. Where do you begin?

The Staff Manual—Blueprint for Success

The first order of business is to produce a staff manual. With the proper information, this manual can provide a working blueprint for producing a successful newspaper. You'll need to do some research to put it together, but you can divide up the work among the staff.

Some members will undoubtedly play a larger role than others, but every person at the meeting should take part in developing the manual. If you have only a few classmates, then each one may have to work on more than one part. If you have many classmates, then two or three could work as a team on each element.

The first element of the manual is the statement of purpose. Why are you publishing this newspaper? What is its purpose, and what is its audience? How do you plan to achieve your purpose and reach your audience? Obviously, you need to know where you're going before you can determine the best way to get there.

The manual should also include an organizational chart that lists the staff positions and who reports to whom. With the chart should be a list of job descriptions or responsibilities. Who's supposed to do what? What will each of the editors' duties be? Who makes the decisions? To whom does a staff member go for answers? Who edits what copy? Who's in charge of planning the various pages? Also important in the manual is a staff directory listing the name, address, and telephone number of every staff member.

Another feature of the staff manual is the publication schedule. If you plan to publish every two weeks, or even once a month, you should spell out your publication and distribution dates for the year. You should also determine how semester finals and holidays will affect your schedule.

Related to the publication schedule is the production schedule. This shows when copy is due for each issue. It also gives deadlines for page design, headlines, photos, captions for photos, and rewrites. The more detailed the schedule, the easier it is for staff members to know what's expected of them. It's also important to know exactly where things stand at each point during the production process.

A valuable addition to your manual is the publication stylebook. The stylebook answers questions like: "Are the names of the months spelled out or abbreviated?" "What about numbers and dates?" You might want to adopt the stylebook found in the appendix.

Another helpful addition to the manual are sample page designs and design information. Look at other school newspapers or professional newspapers. Select pages you like and try to identify the elements you like. Then see if you can adapt them for your newspaper.

A list of format information is another important part of the staff manual. It should show which typefaces will be used for headlines, copy, and captions; the type sizes; and the column widths. If tool lines (thin black rules that are sometimes used between columns of copy) are going to be used, those sizes should also be given. Included with the format information should be a headline schedule. This shows not only the sizes and counts of the headlines you will use, but the counting system as well.

You might also include a **beat sheet** in the staff manual. Every club, organization, and sports team, as well as school officials, such as counselors, principals, deans, and department heads, should be contacted regularly for news and feature story possibilities. The beat sheet is a list of these news sources and the reporters assigned to cover them.

Finally, the staff manual should include an advertising information sheet that lists the advertising deadlines for each issue; the cost of advertising; how the advertising is paid for—in advance or billed; and whether the advertising will be camera-ready or designed by staff members.

There are other items you might like to include, such as a production checklist, reporting and writing tips, a list of commonly misspelled words, a list of commonly used proper names and titles, and whatever else you think you'll need. Your objective is twofold: getting everyone involved in planning the publication and getting that plan on paper.

Assignment 1	Develop an organizational chart and a list of job descriptions for your school newspaper, based upon the number of students in your class. Share your work with your classmates; then compare your chart and list with those of your classmates. Make any modifications you think are needed.

Developing the Staff Manual

At the first planning meeting, assign the various parts of the manual as projects for your classmates. Discuss the general concepts and purpose of each part and then agree to a deadline for having working models completed.

Don't expect perfect plans the first time. You and your classmates may not come up with a workable plan on the first attempt. The important thing is to put the basic elements on paper so that they can be discussed, modified, and tried. In addition to making assignments, you should determine the next meeting time, place, and date. If you need a name for your paper, participants should bring to the next meeting their three choices, in order of preference.

You may not realize it, but you and your classmates are now dealing with planning, organization, personnel management, and time management—concepts you can use for your immediate goals as well as in your future career.

As the manual is being developed and put into action, what happens at future meetings? In addition to developing the manual, you and your classmates should determine intermediate and long-range plans and goals. To do this, you'll need a publication schedule, a **futures** list, and time to plan.

You already have a good idea of what a publication schedule is, but what about the futures list? That's a list of from 100 to 200 features, in-depth, and editorial story ideas that can be developed for your newspaper. At one of the meetings, you and your classmates, using the story idea criteria from Chapter 6, should each bring a list of fifty story ideas. Turn the lists over to one or two participants to compile, cull, and categorize for the next meeting. The master list should have at least 100 ideas.

Assignment 2	Develop a publication and production schedule for your school newspaper. If your school has a biweekly newspaper, develop biweekly schedules; if it is a monthly publication, develop monthly schedules. Avoid copying the sample schedule in the appendix, although you may, if you wish, adapt it to your use.

Assignment 3	Develop a futures list of fifty story ideas for your school newspaper. Share your list with your classmates; then work as a group to select the top 100 or 200 ideas.

Assigning Stories

At the next meeting, spend some time selecting and assigning five, ten, or fifteen ideas for the first issue of your newspaper, using the most timely story ideas. Next pick out and assign a similar number of stories for the second issue and then the third. If your staff is like most student newspaper staffs, you'll publish thirty or more stories in each issue, and so you're just getting started by planning one-third to one-half of the workload for the next three issues.

This advance planning will give you and your classmates time to concentrate on other matters, to work on stories, and to build editing and rewriting time into the production schedule. Among the other matters you'll need to concentrate on are developing and maintaining staff relations, problem solving, and on-going manual development and refinement.

How should a staff be organized? That depends on you and your classmates and your situation. Keep in mind that what works for someone else may not work for you. In addition, people change, situations change, and times change.

Whatever organizational structure you decide to use will be subject to change and should be flexible enough to take advantage of individual situations and the unique talents of staff members. Rather than adopt a specific organizational structure, look at job functions. Then you and your classmates can decide which structure best serves the carrying out of these functions.

The basic functions that must be performed are as follows:

> Story and photo assignments
>
> Gathering information, writing, and rewriting
>
> Editing
>
> Page design
>
> Advertising design and sales
>
> Production (page composition and printout or pasteup)
>
> Promotion, sales, and distribution
>
> Organization and planning
>
> Photography/art
>
> Budget/bookkeeping

That's ten jobs you and others must perform. If you have five staff members, each person will be in charge of two jobs. On the other hand, if you have nineteen classmates, then at least two people can work on each function.

Guidelines for Successful Organization

In setting up your organizational structure, there are five guidelines to follow:

First, one person should be in charge of the overall organization. You and your classmates may decide to have a coeditorship. If so, each should have his or her own area of responsibility. One could be in charge of reporting and editing, and the other in charge of design and production.

Second, one person should be in charge of each function area. Obviously, if there are only five people involved, each person will be in charge of two areas, but if twenty people are involved, then one person can be in charge of one area, with others helping.

Third, each area chief should have at least one backup person. For a five-participant staff, each participant will be in charge of two areas and serve as backup for two other areas. Whether there are five or twenty participants, backups take over in the absence of the area chief. The backups are responsible for knowing what's going on in these areas as well as in their own.

Next, every participant should answer to at least one other person. In the case of an editor-in-chief, he or she should answer to a teacher, an editorial board, a staff panel, or whatever setup you and your classmates think will work best. In case something goes wrong—and things will go wrong—the problem can be evaluated and solved. However, this accountability should never be used to assess blame. Finding someone to blame when things go wrong has never resolved a problem; it only makes it worse. Concentrate, instead, on preventing problems from recurring.

Finally, an organizational chart and a job description should be developed and given to every participant. See the sample flow chart and job description list in the appendix.

After determining the number of positions in your organizational structure, match talents with job responsibilities. The classmate who excels in English should probably be in charge of editing, and a good student artist should be in charge of design. The classmate who is the most organized should perhaps be the editor, managing editor, or be in charge of production. The math whiz would do well in budget/bookkeeping, and the enterprising student who is weak in writing skills could probably do a good job with promotion, sales, and distribution. Now that you have a structure, job positions, and people to fill those jobs, you should develop a production schedule.

Assignment 4	Working with your classmates, develop a publication manual for your school newspaper. If your newspaper staff has a manual, have your teacher obtain a copy and compare it with what you and your classmates have done. If the staff members don't have a manual, ask your teacher to give them a copy of yours and invite them to make specific comments about each part of the manual.

Production Schedules

Deadline. That's one of the most feared words in scholastic journalism because it means work must be completed and turned in by a certain time, or you're dead! Of course you're used to deadlines because you have homework deadlines in your classes. But a school newspaper has a deadline almost every day, and all of them MUST be met. Trying to catch up after missing one or two deadlines can take all the fun out of producing a newspaper.

One of the easiest ways to develop a production schedule is to make a list of all the steps necessary for producing a newspaper, to determine the number of days it will take to complete each step, and then to place each step in order of performance on a calendar, ending with the distribution date.

To achieve this, you might try working backward. For example, if your distribution date is the thirtieth of the month, and it takes two days to print your paper, then your completed pasteup or printout day is the twenty-eighth. If the last job you perform before final printout day is placing down photo captions and headlines, and it takes a day to perform that task, then your headlines and captions need to be placed on the computer by the twenty-seventh. In planning your schedule, don't forget to allow for weekends and holidays.

If it takes the typesetter or the printer two days to complete your captions and headlines, then the deadline for all captions and headlines must be the twenty-fifth. And if it takes a day to write headlines and captions, then all stories and photos must be ready by the twenty-fourth.

If your newspaper is going to be published every two weeks, this means you and your classmates could be working on some phase of two, or even three, issues on the same day. It can be done, but if that is a little frightening, then you might want to consider publishing once a month or every three weeks. You'll find a sample monthly production schedule in the appendix.

Setting up the planning and production of a school newspaper isn't easy. It takes research, work, revision, adjustment, and then more work. However, by following a classic management principle—plan your work, then work your plan—newspaper production and publishing can become a rewarding achievement.

Developing story ideas, researching, interviewing, writing, and rewriting improve your thinking and writing skills and are a source of satisfaction. That satisfaction, however, can also be achieved in a good English composition class. It takes publication—seeing your work in print with your name on it—and the favorable comments from other students to maximize that satisfaction. And when you've also played a major role in the planning and production of the entire newspaper, it brings not only pride but also experience that you'll carry with you throughout your life.

Assignment 5

If your school doesn't have a student newspaper, ask your teacher if your class could start one or publish a single in-class issue. Even if your school has a newspaper, ask your teacher if your class can publish one in-class issue.

Summary

Organization and a staff management plan are essential for operating a successful school newspaper. The best way to organize and plan a smooth operation is to develop a staff manual. The manual should include a production schedule, job descriptions, and other essential information. The best way to put together a manual is to involve everyone on the staff in the process. By using a staff manual, it's possible to assign stories and plan two or three issues in advance. In addition, carrying out the process outlined in the manual can make producing a newspaper a smooth-running and exciting achievement.

13 From Planning to Publication

Just as you need a plan for interviewing and writing, you also need a plan for taking a newspaper from the raw copy stage to printing and distribution.

One of the biggest changes to occur in student publications in recent years is the computerization of the production process. In the past, few schools owned typesetting equipment because the equipment and maintenance were so expensive. In the early 1980s, personal computers became available to student publications. Journalists could utilize the word-processing capabilities and then either send a floppy disk or telecommunicate the information through a modem to a typesetter.

The Desktop Publishing Revolution

In the mid-1980s, the desktop publishing (DTP) revolution began. The basic components of DTP include a computer and monitor, a laser printer, and word processing and desktop publishing software. The most popular software used by school publications includes Adobe PageMaker and Quark XPress. Additional options include scanners, CD-ROM units, tape or disk backup units, modems, and graphic design, typeface, and clip-art software.

DTP allows students to type in their copy, draw the page designs full-size, and then merge the copy and designs to produce, with a laser printer, finished or "camera-ready" pages, ready to go to the printer. Students can also choose to transfer pages on the computer to computer disks and carry the disks to a printer, or, by using a modem, send the pages electronically across a telephone line. In addition to having the finished pages printed, students can also upload (electronically transfer) the pages onto the Internet for people with a computer and modem anywhere in the world to view.

Desktop publishing allows greater control of the mechanical production, greater versatility of design, greater selection of type size and styles, and a significant savings in production costs. Unfortunately, one or two "cutting-edge" computers, support equipment, and software can cost thousands of dollars, putting DTP out of financial reach for many school publications. However, by using older computers, equipment, and software, some schools have come to prefer DTP for producing newspaper pages for publication. In fact, as of the mid-1990s, many high-school publications are being produced using DTP. While the following description of the production process is designed to enable a school to begin publishing a newspaper using DTP, most of these techniques can also be adapted by those already producing a newspaper through DTP or by those using the traditional typesetting and pasteup method.

Joining the Revolution

While DTP provides greater convenience, flexibility, and a professional-looking newspaper made inexpensively, it *isn't* a time-saver. School publications that have switched from typesetting and pasteup methods to DTP have discovered in some instances that DTP actually *increased* the amount of time spent in producing a newspaper: this is because one person composing pages on a computer can't possibly take the place of several people pasting up several pages at one time. For example, if you switch from several staff members simultaneously pasting up four pages to one person composing pages on a single computer, it will take approximately four times as long to produce those same four pages. Keep that in mind when preparing the production schedule discussed in Chapter 12.

Finding a Printer

After determining what equipment and software you'll have for desktop publishing, the next step is to find a printer who can work with a school newspaper. The main factors in selecting a printer are cost and service. Important questions to ask a printer are the following: What are your basic charges for printing a school newspaper? What is the minimum number of copies we must order? What is your charge for halftones? What is your charge for special graphic services, such as screens, reverses, and spot color? Do we need to reserve press time in advance, or can we bring the newspaper in at any time? What would be the turnaround time for printing our newspaper? What steps can we take to save time or money? What additional services do you offer that might benefit us? Do you deliver the newspapers? Do you provide **grid sheets** and if so, is there any charge for them? What is the difference in cost if we provide camera-ready pages or pages on computer disks or telecommunicate our pages through a modem?

You will be relying heavily on the printing company with whom you do business. Printers familiar with school publications can offer invaluable help because of their experience.

Establishing a Budget

The availability of finances, of course, will determine the size and quality of your publications. Although some school administrations fund student publications, most publications rely on outside funding. For this reason, you need to establish a budget.

Whether the newspaper is financed from administrative funding, advertising sales, subscription or per-copy sales, or a combination of these, it's important to estimate the income and expenses as accurately as possible.

Assume, for example, it will cost $1,000 to produce 1,000 copies of an eight-page tabloid newspaper. You know it would be difficult to sell your papers for $1 a copy. The administration can't provide funding, and you don't want to sell subscriptions. This means you and your staff must produce $1,000 in advertising and per-copy sales.

Ideally, you'll want to provide your newspaper free, so everyone will read it. However, it may not be possible to sell enough advertising to pay for the newspaper in full. After conducting an informal survey, you determine that you can probably count on 800 students to purchase the newspaper at 25¢ a copy. This will bring in $200, leaving $800 to be raised from advertising sales.

Setting Advertising Rates

Newspaper advertising is sold in column inches. In advertising language, a 2 × 5 ad is one that is two columns wide and five inches deep for a total of 10 column inches. For example, if your newspaper is tabloid size, and it's laid out in a five-column format, each column will be approximately two inches wide and 13 inches deep.

With a five-column wide by 13-inch deep newspaper, you have a total display area of 65 column inches. However, several pages traditionally contain no advertising. If you decide to omit advertising from the front and back pages of your eight-page newspaper, the editorial page, and the two-page center spread, you are left with only three pages that can carry advertising.

If you decide to limit advertising to no more than 50 percent of any one page, this gives you 32 or 33 column inches of advertising on each of the three pages for a total of 96 or 99 column inches. Divide the $800 you need to raise by the 96 or 99 column inches of advertising space you have available to see what you should charge for advertising.

If you can sell every available column inch of advertising space, you have to charge more than $8 a column inch. In many communities, merchants would refuse to pay that much for a limited-circulation publication.

But if you increase the maximum amount of per-page advertising space to 65 percent and allow advertising on the back page, this gives you 42 column inches or a total available advertising space of 168 column inches.

Dividing the needed $800 by 168, you can price your advertising at $4.76 a column inch. This can be rounded to $5 a column inch—a common cost for school newspaper advertising space. Each page of advertising you add can generate an additional $210.

For this newspaper to be fully financed, you must sell *all* the available advertising space, and you must sell at least 800 copies of the paper at 25¢ a copy. Although this is a simplified overview of budgeting, advertising, and advertising rates, the basic concept works.

Assignment 1

You and your classmates will be publishing a newspaper for a school with 2,000 students and 150 administrators, faculty, and staff. It will be tabloid-size, five columns wide and 15 inches deep. Each of the six issues will have 12 pages. You plan to distribute the paper free of charge and pay for it by selling advertising. Using the following information, determine the per-issue cost of your newspaper. Keep in mind that some costs will occur each issue, while others—such as supplies—will occur only once.

General Supplies

100 pasteup sheets—$15
5 pairs of scissors—$8 each
5 X-Acto knives—$2 each
1 proportion wheel—$3
Printer paper—$30
Billing some supplies—$100
Miscellaneous—$100
5 plastic pica rules—$2 each
Box of 100 X-Acto blades—$7
5 nonreproduction pens—$2 each
Postage for mailing 25 exchange newspapers per issue—$14.50

Photography Costs

24 photos per issue, $5 per photo for film, paper, chemicals	$120

Printing Costs

Minimum printing fee for 2,500 copies per issue	$400
One spot-color, to be used on four pages, per issue	$125
6 page negatives and printing plates, $20 each per issue	$120
24 halftones, $8 each per issue	$192
20 screens, reverses, $8 each per issue	$160

Assignment 2

Using the per-issue cost you've determined in Assignment 1, determine the per-column-inch cost of advertising for your newspaper, based upon the following assumptions.

1. You sell a total of 25 column inches of advertising on 8 of the 12 pages.

2. You sell a total of 25 column inches of advertising on 7 pages plus an additional full page of advertising within the 12 pages.

3. You sell a total of 25 column inches of advertising on 6 pages plus 2 full pages of advertising within the 12 pages.

Assignment 3

To cut the expense of producing your newspaper, you decide to eliminate the spot color, 8 halftones, and 8 screens or reverses:

1. Determine the per-issue cost of your newspaper.

2. Using this cost, determine the per-column-inch cost of advertising based upon selling 25 column inches of advertising on 8 pages.

3. Determine the per-column-inch cost of advertising based upon selling 25 column inches of advertising on 7 pages plus an additional full page of advertising.

4. Determine the per-column-inch cost of advertising based upon selling 25 column inches of advertising on 6 pages plus 2 full pages of advertising.

Determining Newspaper Content

After financing has been worked out, the next step is to determine the content of the newspaper. This is where exchange newspapers are valuable.

You'll find the better school newspapers departmentalize their contents. Their major stories are on page 1, and page 2 is usually reserved for editorials. Page 3 may be a news page. Pages 4 and 5 might be a double-page spread with several stories and photos on a particular subject. Pages 6 and 7 might contain sports, and page 8 could be a features page.

After determining how you want to departmentalize your newspaper, decide how many stories and pictures you think will work best for each page. Often, this is determined by what stories and pictures you have available and which ones you plan to get. As you plan, remember to allow room for headlines and captions.

Getting into Design

Now that the contents have been established, the next step is to design the pages. Again, quality exchange papers can be a valuable source of ideas. Look for designs you like, but do not plagiarize. Rather, take a concept you like and modify it for your particular situation.

The best school newspapers today use what's known as **modular, or block, design.** Type and illustrations are thought of as a series of horizontal blocks running across the page. Each story is squared off and fitted together with others to form a page or a spread of two pages that is visually pleasing.

Both commercial and school newspapers use modular design for several reasons. It has a simple, clean, well-organized look. Clutter confuses the reader; a neat modular design invites the reader to spend time reading the newspaper.

Another important advantage is that modular design makes the production process easier. Modules can be inserted and pulled from a page design without affecting the surrounding modules. This makes story, art, and photo substitutions much easier.

Still another advantage is that modules allow the packaging of related stories, photos, and artwork within a border. As you look at modular newspapers, notice how many of the stories are surrounded by a thin, black rule forming a box. The reader can easily see that all elements in the box are related.

Standards and Measurement

Before you begin designing your newspaper, you need to know certain measurements and guidelines.

Copy, before it's typed on the computer, is usually measured in numbers of words. First you must determine the number of words per inch in typeset copy before you can tell how inches of space your stories will require.

Utilizing the typeface and size of type you plan to use for body copy, set several inches of copy in the various column widths you plan to use in your newspaper. Then count the number of words in each inch. If every story turned in includes a word count, you can easily estimate how much space each story will take.

Although vertical measurements in a newspaper are generally given in inches, often they are measured in points and lines. A point is a unit of vertical measurement, usually referring to type size. There are 72 points in an inch. This means eight lines of 8-point body type with 1-point **leading** (spacing between each line) will take up one inch of vertical space.

Horizontal space in a newspaper is usually measured in picas and columns. There are six picas to an inch, and since columns are measured in picas, a 12-pica column would measure two inches wide.

Here's a simple table to help you remember the relationship of points, picas, and inches.

72 points	=	1 inch
6 picas	=	1 inch
12 points	=	1 pica

Determining Format

Before setting the type standards you'll use for your newspaper, you must determine the dimensions of the newspaper itself. A full-sized newspaper, such as *USA Today,* is known as a **broadsheet** and is approximately 15 inches wide by 24 inches long. A **tabloid** paper, like the *Christian Science Monitor,* is half the size and is approximately 12 inches wide and anywhere from 13 to 15 inches long. A mini-tabloid is half the size of a tabloid and is approximately 8½ inches wide by 11 inches long, like *Time Magazine.*

A broadsheet format usually has six or seven columns across; a tabloid format, four or five columns; and a mini-tabloid, three or four columns.

If you're working with a tabloid newspaper, your news space might be designed on a four-column format, with each column measuring 14 picas wide, and with one pica of space between columns. Deciding on a four-column format doesn't mean everything will be set 14 picas wide, nor does it prevent selling advertising on a five-column basis. It's possible—even advantageous—to vary the column width of type and photos, as long as the total package begins and ends on a column line.

Headline typefaces, sizes, and leading also must be selected. Most typesetting companies are helpful in giving suggestions for attractive typefaces for body copy and headlines.

For body copy, you'll probably want to use a 9- or 10-point type, with 1 or 2 points of leading. Headline type should include a mixture of bold and light or bold and italic and should be available in various sizes. Leading for headlines normally ranges from 2 to 3 points, depending on the size of the type.

Guidelines for Design

Now you're ready to look at some principles of design. Remember to work with rectangles, and keep your page design simple. Designing a page is like building a simple puzzle out of rectangles. You'll also save time and frustration if you design your pages on paper first and then transfer the finished designs and measurements to the computer.

Every newspaper needs a **nameplate,** which always appears on the front page, traditionally at the top. The nameplate gives the name of the newspaper and the school and lists the school address, date of publication, and volume and issue numbers. In some instances, it also carries information on features inside the newspaper.

All newspapers use **folio lines** and **page numbers** on each page. Folio lines list the newspaper name, date, and sometimes general page contents, such as news, sports, opinion, advertising, or features. Folio lines and page numbers are found either at the top or bottom of each page.

Every newspaper should have a **masthead** or **staff box.** This gives the complete address and telephone number of the school, advertising rates, press organization memberships, and awards won by the newspaper. It also lists the editors and reporters on the staff. The staff box usually appears within the first four pages of the newspaper or on the editorial page.

After you've designed and agreed upon your nameplate, folio lines, and masthead, it's best to input them into the computer; then save them in separate files so that with minor changes, they can be used again in each issue during the year.

Each page should have **a center of visual interest (CVI)**—a place that draws the reader's attention. This can be a large appealing photo, a headline, a piece of artwork, or a combination of these. It should be the dominant element and at least one-and-a-half or two times larger than any other element on the page. Often, the CVI is placed in the upper-right corner of an odd-numbered page, and in the upper-left corner of an even-numbered page. If you have two unrelated photos for a page, one should be horizontal and one vertical. Two or more related photos should be clustered together.

When designing a page, don't divide it in the middle, either horizontally or vertically. Always have at least one module that breaks or stops the division line. A page can be divided into thirds, horizontally or vertically, but don't do that on every page. One of the most effective modular page designs uses an E-shaped layout.

Avoid **tombstoning** headlines, unrelated photographs, or artwork. *Tombstoning* means running headlines or unrelated photos adjacent to each other. From a design standpoint, tombstoning can put too much weight in one area of the page. And in the case of headlines, it can cause a reader to read two

Sample Nameplates

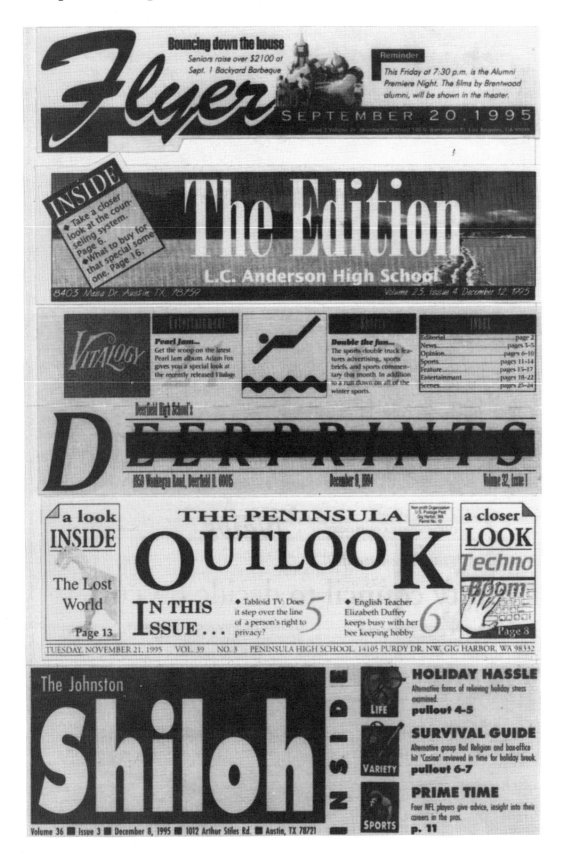

headlincs as one. In the case of photos, the reader might think that unrelated photos are somehow related. You can avoid bumping heads by contrasting the size and type of heads or by placing one of the headlines and its accompanying story inside a box. Whenever possible, use boxes, photos, or artwork to separate headlines.

Many papers today use what's known as **downstyle headlines.** Capitalize the first letter of the first word and the first letter of proper nouns in a headline.

Try to use at least one graphic device on each page. This can be a boxed story and headline, a quote from a story in large bold type between two rules, large initial letters placed at the beginning and in several strategic paragraphs to break up gray areas, a light screen over a story and headline, or a piece of artwork within a story. But be careful not to clutter a page with too many graphic devices. One or two on a page is enough.

As a general rule, stories seven inches or longer should be run horizontally across two or more columns, and shorter stories should be run vertically in one column. Several short stories can be packaged and run vertically down one column or horizontally over several columns, as long as it's obvious the stories go together. A common way to group several brief stories is to give each its own headline, then place them together in a box.

Readers normally associate a story next to a photo with a photo. If you run a story above or below a photo, you imply a relationship, whether it exists or not. By boxing the photo along with the story and headline or partially surrounding the photo with copy, you can avoid confusion. If you choose to partially surround a photo with the story, it's best to run the copy on the left side and bottom of the photo.

If you have only one photo for a page, place it on the top half of the page. Then balance the page by placing a screened story, artwork, or a story with a large headline in the lower half of the page.

Avoid placing photos, artwork, and boxed or screened stories next to ads because they compete for the reader's eye. Place your advertising in blocks across the bottom of a page, rather than up the side. Try to arrange the ads so they are spread evenly across the bottom of the page, leaving a rectangular space for your copy and photos.

There are many design guidelines that can help you produce a professional quality, reader-pleasing newspaper, but these basic principles can put you on the road to design success.

Assignment 4

Draw miniature page dummies; position the ads, and then calculate the newspaper's advertising revenue in the following situations. Except where noted, distribute the ads as evenly as possible across the bottom of the pages.

1. An 8-page tabloid newspaper, with each page having five columns that are 15 inches deep. The advertising rate is $5 a column inch. Ads should not be placed on the front page or editorial page.

No. of ads	Ad Size	No. of ads	Ad size
1	5 × 8	2	3 × 8
2	2 × 8	3	3 × 5
3	2 × 5		

2. A 12-page tabloid newspaper, with each page having four columns that are 15 inches deep. The advertising rate is $3.50 a column inch, and you do not want ads on the front, back, or editorial pages. You may use two full pages for ads.

No. of ads	Ad Size	No. of ads	Ad size
1	4 × 15	2	4 × 8
2	2 × 8	2	2 × 7
1	2 × 5	1	2 × 3½
1	2 × 3	2	2 × 2½
7	2 × 2	2	2 × 1
2	1 × 4	17	1 × 2

Beginning Design with the Front Page

Construct a layout dummy, or rough plan, for your paper. Begin with the front page. First, you will need to design the nameplate, folio lines, and staff box. Using ideas from exchange newspapers or the commercial press, sketch out sample nameplates, folio lines, and staff boxes for your newspaper. Once you and your staff decide what you like, draw each element to size.

Next, determine what stories and photos will be the best ones for the front page. For a tabloid paper, there should be no more than five or six stories. By discussing newsworthiness and the probable length of each story and the size of each photo with your staff, you can estimate the space each element will take and where it will be placed—before assignments are made.

After the nameplate, sketch your dominant element on the page. If it's a photo with an accompanying story, place the package in the upper-left or upper-right corner. Take the remaining elements, visualize them as rectangles, and then piece your puzzle together. After a few sketches, you'll come up with a pleasing design.

After completing your front-page design, start on page 2, which might be the editorial page. Place the folio lines first, then the dominant element, and, finally, the remainder of the pieces. In your sketch, make sure you allow room for headlines and photo captions.

Design the rest of the pages in the same way, drawing detailed page dummies as you go; then transfer the page designs to the computer.

Assignment 5

Design a nameplate for your school newspaper. It should be no more than two inches deep. It should include the name of your newspaper, the name and address of your school, the volume, issue number, and date.

Sample Layout Dummy

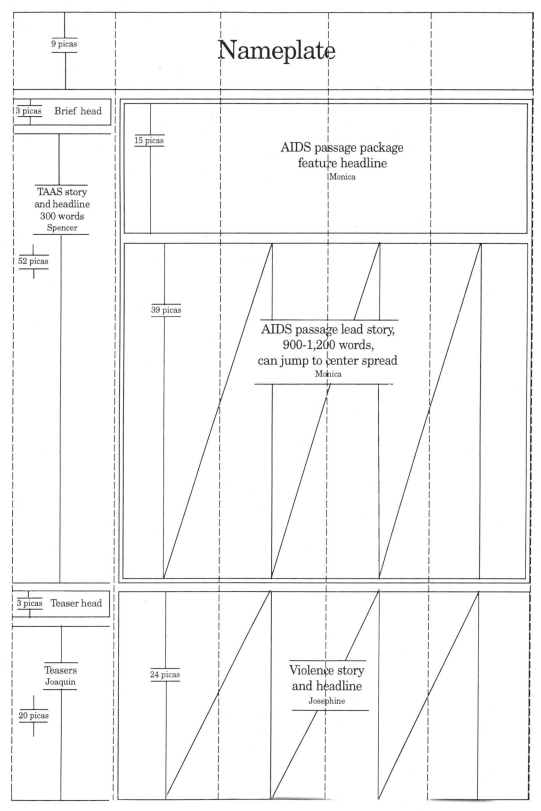

9 picas

Nameplate

3 picas   Brief head

15 picas

AIDS passage package
feature headline
Monica

TAAS story
and headline
300 words
Spencer

52 picas

39 picas

AIDS passage lead story,
900-1,200 words,
can jump to center spread
Monica

3 picas   Teaser head

Teasers
Joaquin

24 picas

Violence story
and headline
Josephine

20 picas

Sample Page Layout

W.B. Ray High School
1002 Texan Trail
Corpus Christi, TX 78411

EL☆TEJANO

Volume 45
Issue 2
October 13, 1995

Briefs

◆ TAAS Testing

BY SPENCER WILLIAMS

Juniors and seniors who fail a portion of the TAAS have previously been sent to the cafeteria or library to retest; however, this year students will retake the test in classrooms, forcing some teachers to hold classes, during the three days the tests will be taken, at other locations throughout the school, such as the library and cafeteria.

The tests will be taken from Oct. 23-26 in the history wing and in the math rooms near the fine arts wing.

Principal Dr. Bruce Scott said the retesting technique was based on research. "Students who take the TAAS in small settings do better than when taken in a large setting," Scott said.

Counselors from Ray and CCISD officials will be administering the tests. Scott said he wanted to give students every advantage, even if it required a change in meeting place.

Many teachers, however, do not like this idea. They believe that the switch is inconvenient. "They have already had the benefit of small group testing, and it did not help," history teacher Ann Couser said.

United States government and world geography teacher Scott Baxter also believes that the policy will not work. "It worked when they took the retest in the library; I don't think these rooms would provide a difference for these students," he said.

Many teachers believe that being grouped in the cafeteria with other classes will be a waste of instructional time. They believe that it will be hard, if not impossible, to hold the attention of their students.

Inside

Living & DYING

One thing that is made clear is how death, as love, is blind and knows no color and no religion. "I'm dying, but you are too, just in a different form. We're not that different," a resident said.

Passage provides haven for dying patients

BY MONICA DAVILA

I walked into the Passage with mixed emotions. A small, naive part of me expected to find a house full of the *Real World's* Pedro Zamoras, ready and able to talk about life and philosophies. The other part of me expected to find a house full of doctors and nurses, basically a nursing home.

The Passage is a house where AIDS patients go who are diagnosed with six months or

A lot of people don't understand how hard it gets.
--Passage resident

less to live. Real people, not statistics or television personalities, live here. These people are mothers, fathers, sisters, and brothers. Just like us, they once had an optimistic future full of goals.

"I had my whole life planned," one resident said. "I

had my house paid for by the time I was 24. I was a big waste. All I did was work. Now I'm too sick to do what I want."

On the outside, the Passage looks like just any other house. There are no big signs in front that mark the building. It is just a house. Most people don't even know it's there.

The house's atmosphere is a mixture of sorrow and hope. These emotions may seem different, but in reality they are quite similar. With pain always comes hope. If you never hurt for something, you would never hope for anything.

"AIDS is like any other fatal disease, except this one has no cure, yet," another resident said.

Not everyone with AIDS comes to the Passage. Some people just need a home environment during the final months of their life.

"A lot of people don't understand how bad it gets," one resident said. "I used to be 150 pounds. Now, I'm 120, maybe less. That's what the disease does."

Others need the around-the-clock care provided by the Passage. Some go blind in their final stages. Others have families that can no

longer take care of them. Sometimes their families just abandon them.

"The house is a safe place, especially for people whose families can't care for them. Some people don't have families," a resident said. "I don't have a family. So I came here."

The people who come into the Passage are not all without family. The staff becomes their family, even if they have another family somewhere else. Some families can't handle taking care of them. Others think if you just ignore it, it will go away.

The Passage was originally called 'David's House'. David founded the house in the late 80s. He was dying of AIDS and knew that many AIDS victims needed a place to go.

The Passage is free to the residents and is the only house like it in the country. The only requirement to get in is to have been diagnosed by a doctor with six months or less to live.

Though most of the people who come into the house are men, there is a rising number of women with HIV or AIDS.

"There has only been three women in the past year who have come, but that is unfortunately changing. " Mike Hoppings, a caregiver said.

The world inside this house is so different from the judgemental world we live in. The caregivers are inspiring.

It's a very deadly disease. It's not worth playing to get it.
--Passage resident

They give everything they have to the people within the Passage. They become their mothers and fathers. They put aside their lives and extend themselves to people they don't even know. They cook for them, make sure they eat well, and help with their medicines.

"I just wanted to do something to do with AIDS," Hoppings said. "I felt I wanted to help out with a problem."

Not only do the caregivers give these people physical care, but also emotional care. They talk to them about whatever, whenever.

See PASSAGE, page 6

Violence increases since closed campus policy

Security guards report increase of violent acts during lunch

BY JOSEPHINE CORPUS

The lunch shifts have recently turned from a time to eat to a time to spot the latest fight.

There has been an increase in violence during lunch since the campus was closed and students were not allowed to leave for lunch.

"We've had a lot [of fights], but I've only had to break up two," security guard Octavio Chavero said.

Sergeant Timothy Martin, hired from the sheriff's dept., also says there has been an increase. "I am only here two days a week and have had to break up four or five fights," he said.

Sometimes the police officers or security guards have the chance to control the students before they start to fight. "I've been able to catch most fights before they begin," Martin said.

On the other hand, the students occasionally finish fighting before the officers or guards show up. "By the time the security guards get there, the [students] have just stopped fighting," Assistant Principal Yolanda Boyd said.

Fights have taken place in locations other than the cafeteria "Fights are usually outside in places such as the gazeboes, portables, tennis courts, and the foyer," Boyd said.

Breaking up a fight can be dangerous, according to Martin. "In a crowd, I have to break them up and watch my back," he said.

Weapon involvement in a fight is also a problem. A student was using a letter opener in a fight at the beginning of the year, according to Gaddis.

The security guards have had problems mainly with underclassmen. "The majority are ninth graders and a few sophomores," Boyd said.

Students have their own opinions about the fights. "I think they are childish and stupid," junior Robin Botello said.

Some even have their own opinions about the students involved in the fights. "I think [the students] like to cause trouble just to get attention," junior Cathy Garza said.

The punishments of the students are decided by their assistant principal and include parental conferences, suspension, and expulsion. "Usually we give them three days suspension," Assistant Principal Tom Gaddis said. "I think [violence] will start going down because of student removals."

Assignment 6 Design a modular front page for the following newspapers, using the listed elements, allowing space for headlines.

1. A 5-column by 15-inch newspaper, with a 5-column by 2-inch nameplate. Contents: a 12-inch student council story, plus a 3-column by 6-inch photo, including the caption; a 15-inch school-annex construction story; a 10-inch story on next year's school calendar.

2. A 4-column by 15-inch newspaper, with a 4-column by 2-inch nameplate. Contents: a 10-inch story on a new video class, with a 1-column by 3-inch photo, including the caption; an 18-inch school budget story, including a 2-column by 1½-inch enlarged quote as a graphic device; a 10½-inch story on student testing results; a 3-column by 3½-inch graph showing the results of a survey on teen recreation habits.

3. A 5-column by 15-inch newspaper, with a 5-column by 1½-inch nameplate. Contents: a 5-column by 1½-inch "What's Inside" promotional graphic that spotlights three special features in the newspaper; a 10-inch story on a mock convention; an 8-inch story on a new assistant principal, plus a 3-column by 5-inch photo, including caption; a 9-inch story on asbestos removal; a 2-column by 4-inch photo of a movie star visiting the school, including caption.

Assigning Stories and Photos

Now that your pages are designed and the content determined, it's time to assign stories and photos. Many newspaper staffs estimate word counts for each major story and assign word counts with the stories. At the same time, they determine the size and content of photos and assign them. Deadlines for stories and photos are also given.

After the stories are turned in, edited, and returned to the writers for rewriting, if necessary, and after final rewrites and editing have taken place, the stories are listed on a **log sheet.** This keeps track of all parts of the paper, along with column widths and approximate length in inches.

At this point, some staffs write the headlines and then type both stories and headlines into the computer. Most staffs, however, type and place their stories in the computer before writing and placing the headlines. In either case, it's important to establish a smooth copy flow and to type copy into the computer as it's ready.

Selecting and Editing Photos

While the copy is being keyboarded (typed) into the computer, it's a good idea to begin choosing photos for the newspaper. All photos should be selected on the basis of their news value and impact. Each photo should tell a story. It should be in focus, featuring sharp detail and good contrast. There should also be at least one recognizable, identifiable person in the photo, and unless it's what is known as a **mug shot,** a photo of someone's face, the person or people in the photo should be doing something identifiable.

Too often, school photojournalists practice "assassination photography." The subjects are lined up against a wall and their picture is shot. Reader interest in photographs is much higher when the subjects are in action, whether it's in the senior play, the 100-meter dash, or simply eating ice cream. There should also be a visual center of interest in each photo—an action or feature that draws the reader's eye into the photo. This means faces should be as large as possible, but not so large that they detract from the action.

Finally, make sure all unnecessary areas in the photo are eliminated. It is up to you or another staff member to eliminate the problem areas. This is called **cropping,** and it's usually done with a ruler and grease pencil to define the desirable area. The next step is sizing the pictures. This is accomplished by using a **proportion wheel.** Consisting of two circular disks of plastic—one smaller than the other—a proportion wheel is used to compare the width and depth of the photo with the width and depth of the space it will take up in the newspaper.

Find the depth measurement on the outer disk that matches the depth of the newspaper photo space. Directly across from that measurement you'll see the depth the photo must have in order to fill the space. If that depth doesn't match the depth of the actual photo, you'll need to crop the photo so the measurements will match. Try to avoid cropping a photo that is already cropped well. When the measurements match, the small window on the inner disk will give the percentage of enlargement or reduction needed to make the photo fit the newspaper space. This percentage needs to be noted for the printer.

Later, the printer will make **halftones** of your photos, photographing each picture through a screen that breaks the picture into dots and makes it possible to reproduce it in print. You may wish to have the finished halftones returned so that you can use them in creating what's known as a "camera-ready" newspaper.

On the other hand, if you have access to a photo scanner and software, you'll want to first edit and scan in your own photos and then place them on the pages in the computer before printing out your pages. Not only does this give you greater selection and control over your photos and sizes, it results in a significant savings as well, since you'll eliminate halftone charges.

Writing Photo Captions

If you send your photos to the printer, you need to write captions before sending the photos. Or you might wish to photocopy the photos, so that captions can be written while the photos are at the printer.

Captions must identify the major, visually prominent people in the photo. Captions also must tell what is happening in the photo, but they should never tell the obvious.

For example, if students are shown eating ice cream, the caption shouldn't read, "Several students are shown eating ice cream." Rather, develop the newsworthiness by explaining why they're eating ice cream. Caption information should come from the photographer.

The best captions tell the reader something the photo doesn't show and give the results or importance of the action. The caption should be thought of as a mini-story that explains why a particular photograph appears in the newspaper. That means it should answer the **Five Ws** and the **H** of journalism.

Avoid beginning captions with people's names or "ing" words. And study captions in national magazines or metropolitan newspapers for excellent examples.

The final step in preparing captions is to type them into the computer and then to place them on their respective pages. As a general rule, captions should be placed the same width as the photo. But if a photo is more than two columns wide, the caption should be placed half the photo width, less one pica, to appear in two columns for better readability.

Proceeding to Final Printout

When placing all of your elements—copy, headlines, photos, captions, graphics, and so forth—on the pages, you'll most likely discover that your elements don't fit exactly as you've planned them to on the page dummies. By making minor adjustments, however, you can make the elements fit. These adjustments include deleting words and lines or paragraphs of copy, rewording headlines or making them larger or smaller, resizing or substituting photographs, adding or eliminating stories or photos, and rewriting captions or copy. However, avoid "squeezing" headlines and do not change the size or leading of body copy.

Once pages are composed on the computer, the staff can print them out, check them carefully for errors, and then use the marked-up printouts to make final corrections on the computer. Unless an 11 × 17-inch or larger printer is used, tabloid-sized or broadsheet pages will need to be "tiled" out on several 8½ × 11-inch pages. With a little practice, staff members will be able to print out individual blocks of stories and headlines to place over the "breaks" that occur in tiling.

After corrections have been made, final pages can be printed or tiled out and placed on the pasteup sheets. Although some staffs use rubber cement or spray adhesive, many find that wax is preferable. The advantage of using wax is that pages can be pulled up and put down again without damaging the copy. When the pages are pasted down—particularly when tiling is used—carefully check to ensure that everything is straight and that all corrections have been made. Along with the pages, send instructions for the printer on the number of copies to be printed, the type of paper you want to use, and any special information regarding spot color, screens, or halftone placement.

The sale of the newspaper should be promoted at least two or three days in advance by using posters, the school public-address or closed-circuit television system, and by word of mouth. Tantalizing your audience with bits of information about the newspaper's various stories can help increase sales when the paper is finally distributed.

When the bundles of newspapers are delivered or picked up, make sure your camera-ready pages have been enclosed as well. After distribution, each staff member must be alert for reader reactions. Such information is invaluable for planning the next issue.

If you've never been involved in producing and publishing a school newspaper, you're in for a pleasant surprise. Chances are your classmates will be impressed with your product and will tell you so. When you hear the praise and compliments of friends, teachers, and others, you'll realize that all your efforts have been worthwhile—and that you're now a journalist.

Summary

The steps for turning copy into a finished newspaper can seem long and complicated, but operating according to a set plan can save you time, money, and anxiety.

Desktop publishing has greatly simplified the publication process for schools. The use of computers, DTP software, and a laser printer eliminates the pasteup process entirely. Through the proliferation of computers in schools or donations of computers and software from local businesses, most newspaper staffs are now delivering their pages to the printer "camera-ready." Many are even using modems to place their newspapers on the Internet, so that they are available to people throughout the world.

The major steps in producing a newspaper include securing the use of computers, DTP software, and a laser printer; finding a printing company that can provide helpful information and handle your business; determining the newspaper's format and mechanical standards; establishing type, copy, and page standards; and setting advertising rates that meet the budget.

In addition, you'll need to set up procedures for page designing, photo editing and cropping; caption and headline writing; copy preparation and keyboarding; and page composition. Once a workable production system is in place, these procedures will produce a quality publication of which your staff—and the entire school—can be proud.

Glossary

Advance: A story written about an upcoming event.

Angle: The point of view taken in developing and reporting a story.

Attribution: Indicating the source of information or quotations.

Beat sheet: A list of persons, clubs, and organizations and the reporters who cover them.

Bleed: Running a photo into the margin or edge of a page.

Boldface type: A typeface that is darker than the regular typeface.

Brainstorming: Generating new ideas in a group setting.

Brite: A short, humorous feature story.

Broadsheet: A traditional-size newspaper that measures anywhere from 15 inches wide and 24 inches long to 14 inches wide and 23 inches long.

Camera-ready: Newspaper pages, ready for the printer to photograph and print.

Caption: Information describing the people or explaining the action in a photo.

CD-ROM: An acronym that stands for *Compact Disk-Read Only Memory*. It's used in desktop publishing to provide hundreds of typefaces or clip art.

Censor: To remove information considered objectionable.

Cliché: An expression that has been overused.

Clip art: Drawings, art work, or cartoons used to illustrate stories or provide graphic appeal to pages.

Copyright: The protection of printed material preventing reproduction without permission.

Cropping: Improving the impact of a photograph by eliminating unnecessary clutter.

Deck head: Two or more lines of headline, usually a secondary headline accompanying a larger primary headline.

Defamation: Damaging the reputation of a person or organization through libel or slander.

Desktop publishing (DTP): Using a computer and specially designed software to typeset and design a publication.

Downstyle: Capitalizing only the first letter of the first word and proper nouns in a headline.

Drop head: A smaller, secondary headline placed below the primary headline.

Dummy sheet: Paper ruled vertically in inches and horizontally in columns, on which preliminary plans for a page can be drawn.

Editorial: A written article of opinion in a newspaper.

Ethics: Standards of conduct for journalists.

Feature: An informally written story emphasizing background or entertainment rather than news.

Five Ws and the H: The who, what, when, where, why, and how that make up the basis for most new stories.

Flow chart: A printed organizational structure showing lines of authority and responsibility, along with the relationship between offices within the organization.

Fold: The place where a newspaper is usually folded in half.

Folio line: Information, usually at the top of each page, with the page number, date, publication name, and sometimes the content of the page.

Format: The size, number of columns, and general makeup of a publication.

Futures list: A list of feature stories and news articles for possible future use in a newspaper.

Grid sheets: Pages provided by a printer containing guidelines for pasting up newspaper copy or for placing printed-out pages on for delivery to the printer.

Gutter: The space between columns or between facing pages.

Halftone: The result of photographing a picture through a screen, which breaks the image into dots and makes it possible to reproduce the photograph in print.

Hard copy: A typed or computer printout of material.

Keyboarding: Typing copy into a computer.

Kicker: A short, secondary headline placed above a larger primary headline.

Laser Printer: A reproduction device utilizing a laser beam to print material, comparable in detail to offset printing.

Lead: The first sentence or two of a story that tells the reader what the story is about.

Leading: The amount of space between lines of type.

Libel: Damaging the reputation of an individual or organization by printing false information.

Log sheet: A list of stories and their approximate lengths.

Masthead: A listing of staff members, positions, and essential information, such as address and ad rates. It's also referred to as a staff box.

Mini-tab: A magazine size publication, approximately $8\frac{1}{2}$ inches wide by 11 inches long.

Modem: A device used for the electronic transfer of material from one computer to another over a telephone line.

Module: A variable rectangular space used in designing newspaper pages.

Nameplate: A design feature that tells the name of the newspaper, address, date, volume, and issue number. It appears on the front page, usually at the top.

Nut graf: A brief paragraph that explains the significance of a story.

Obscenity: A word or statement that offends people's sense of morality or decency. From a legal standpoint, something that appeals solely to prurient interests.

Offset: A printing process in which the inked impressions from a printing plate are transferred–or offset–onto a rubber roller and then onto a sheet of paper.

Package: Related material joined into a visually organized grouping.

Page dummy: The hand-drawn guideline for planning a newspaper page.

Pasteup: The cutting and pasting of type, headlines, and photos on a page to produce camera-ready material.

Pica: A unit of measurement, equal to $\frac{1}{6}$ of an inch.

Plagiarism: Claiming or using someone else's idea or work as your own.

Plaintiff: Someone who files suit in a court of law.

Point: A unit of measurement in type, equal to $\frac{1}{72}$ of an inch.

Primary head: A headline that is larger and bolder than its accompanying headline.

Proofing: Carefully checking copy or typeset material for errors.

Reverse: The printing of white type on a black surface, instead of the usual black type on a white surface.

Satire: The use of ridicule or sarcasm to poke fun at the faults of an individual, organization, or society in general.

Scanner: An electronic device used to "read" or convert photographs, art, or printed material and electronically place it in a computer file.

Screens: Shades of ink coverage usually measured in percentages, such as 20 or 40 percent, that produce a lighter shade.

Secondary head: A headline that is smaller and lighter than its accompanying headline.

Seditious libel: A term used in colonial America to indicate printed material that could stir up rebellion or unrest.

Sizing: Determining the proportional enlargement or reduction of a photograph to fit the allotted space in a publication.

Software: Programs that enable a computer to perform specific functions.

Spot color: The use of colored ink in certain areas of a newspaper.

Tabloid: A newspaper measuring approximately 11 inches wide by 14 to 16 inches deep.

Telecommunicating: Electronically transferring material on a computer or a disk to another computer over a telephone line.

Tile: In desktop publishing, printing oversized publication pages in sections, or tiles, on more than one page.

Tombstoning: Placing headlines of similar size beside each other, making them appear as though they were one headline.

Transition: Words or phrases that move the reader smoothly from one paragraph to the next.

Typeface: The characteristics of a particular style of type.

Uploading: Electronically transferring information from a computer file to the internet so that others can have access to that information.

Appendix

Copyediting Symbols

How They Are Used	What They Mean
For the sixth time	paragraph
state highway. No new figures	new paragraph
state highway. No new figures	
game of the season.	no paragraph; run on
While the Trojans	
In colorado	capitalize
Next to The store	lowercase
Rather than go to	delete a letter
During the the late	delete a word
Withoqout having a	delete and close up
Defi nitely forgiving	close up
From the begining	insert a letter
Shortly after votes	insert a word
at 407 Rapid Street	abbreviate
in her 8th grade class	spell out
a total of sixty-seven	set in numerals
But when the time came	transpose letters
how often police the called	transpose words
It wasn't exactly without	separate words
without their support	ignore copy mark; leave it alone
by Winston Salem	set in boldface
In The Edition last week	set in italics
for the end of time.	set flush left
Photo by Steve Barnes	set flush right
A statement of opinion	center copy
more	copy continues
30 or # or endit	end of copy
Until now the best	insert comma
after hours That's when	insert period
He said, I didn't know	insert quotation marks
Thats what they have	insert apostrophe
She's a kind hearted	insert hyphen

Stylebook

A stylebook does not deal with matters of literary expression. Instead, it presents rules that, when followed, lead to consistency in punctuation, abbreviation, capitalization, and spelling. These rules are somewhat arbitrary. A reporter is not wrong because he or she has spelled out, rather than abbreviated, the word *September*. He or she has simply failed to follow current journalistic practice.

Large daily newspapers, like the *New York Times* and the *Chicago Tribune*, have their own stylebooks. Many others rely on the stylebook published jointly by the Associated Press and United Press International. The main value of any stylebook is that it saves time. A reporter or an editor does not need to ponder or analyze comma usage, for example. He or she only needs to look it up in the stylebook and follow the rule.

Abbreviations

- Spell out organization names on first reference, but abbreviate them in subsequent references.

    Students Against Drunk Driving (SADD)

    Exceptions: PTA, FBI, other organizations widely recognized by their initials

- Abbreviate months with five or more letters when used in dates.

    Oct. 4, 1998

    July 17, 1996

- Abbreviate *avenue, boulevard,* and *street* when writing a specific address. Spell out words such as *drive, circle, road, terrace,* or *alley.*

    1208 Wilderness Blvd.

    down on Lamar Road

- Do not abbreviate units of measurement.

    The new stage will be 15 feet deeper than the old one.

    Exception: 35mm film

- Do not use the abbreviation *etc.* in news stories.

Capitalization

- Capitalize all proper nouns.

    Harrison High School

- Capitalize all titles preceding names but not those after names.

    General Manager Richard Lytle

    Edwina Sharpe, vice president for administration

- Capitalize names of languages and courses with proper names.

    English

    Introduction to Theater

    algebra

- Capitalize independent clauses following a colon.

    His speech had one main point: All students should try to improve themselves and their environment.

- Capitalize *east, northwest, south, midwest* when they refer to a region, not when they refer to a direction.

    the East

    Go east.

- Capitalize all references to a personal deity. Capitalize words such as *Bible, Koran,* and *Old Testament* when referring to sacred writings. Lowercase *biblical*. Lowercase *bible* when referring to a nonreligious book of authority.

    We visited a shrine to the Buddha.

    He quoted from the Old Testament.

    The stylebook should be your copyediting bible.

Names and Titles

- Use first and last names in first mention of student and staff members. In later references, use last names and titles only.

    Dr. Dolores Ebert (first mention)

    Dr. Ebert (later reference)

- Designate students by class before the name. Designate teachers or staff members with a descriptive title.

    Senior Tany Coker

    Ruth Radomski, biology teacher

- Do not use *Mr., Mrs., Miss,* or *Ms.* unless needed to differentiate among people with the same last name.

    Mr. and Mrs. Jones

Numbers

- Spell out numbers under 10 and use numerals for number 10 and above.

    Scholarships have been awarded to five students.

    The science club has grown to include 40 students.

- Spell out approximate figures.

  Almost two thousand people attended the rally.

- Spell out fractions less than one.

  Three-fourths

- Use a comma in numbers of four or more figures.

  2,215 books

- Use figures for dollar and cent amounts.

  $15

  33¢

- Use figures for all temperatures except zero. Use the word *minus,* not a minus sign, to indicate negative numbers.

  With the wind chill, the temperature reached minus 25.

  The temperature dropped to zero.

- Do not use zeros with even hours or dollar amounts.

  7 P.M.

  $15

- Use words and numerals for very large numbers.

  $15 million

- Spell out and capitalize *first* through *ninth* when used as street names. Use figures for 10th and above.

  Third Avenue

  61st Street

- No not begin a sentence with a number unless absolutely necessary. Then spell out the number.

  The year 1995 was a good one.

  Three hundred and fifty-one students graduated.

Punctuation

Periods

- Use periods with time designations *A.M.* and *P.M.*

- Use a period before decimal fractions.

  79.9 percent

- Place periods inside parentheses only when the parenthetical material is a complete sentence. Place periods outside parentheses when the parenthetical material is part of a sentence.

  (The Council has the power to change minor regulations.)

  Myeko Sasaki won the writing competition (sponsored by the Jaycees).

- Use a series of periods—an ellipsis—to indicate an omission of words. Treat the ellipsis as a three-letter word constructed of three periods and two spaces.

  "We the people . . . for the United States of America."

  The arms treaty is a good one. . . .

Commas

- Use a comma to separate two independent clauses.

  The concert drew a large crowd, and the band was inspired.

- Do not use a comma before a conjunction in a simple series.

  Red, white and blue are America's colors.

- Use commas to set off nonessential clauses and phrases, including titles after names.

  Howard Woerner, who is our biology teacher, won the competition.

- Use a comma after a dependent clause beginning a sentence.

  After the bell rang, the class left.

- Use a comma to precede a direct quote in quotation marks.

  Larry said, "Our bowling team really had to work for the championship."

- Use a comma to indicate a minor break in thought.

  Wait three seconds, then run.

- Use a comma to separate a month or date from the year.

  January, 1997

  June 21, 1998

Colons

- Use a colon before long lists or long quotations.
- Capitalize independent clauses following a colon.

  To restate the problem: Is the community or the state responsible for quality education?

Semicolons

- Use the semicolon sparingly in news stories.
- Use a semicolon to separate independent clauses not joined by a conjunction.

  Jim played tuba; Carolyn played flute.

- Use a semicolon to separate clauses of a compound sentence that are joined by words such as *therefore, however, nevertheless,* or *otherwise.*

  He must turn in his paper; otherwise, he will fail.

- Use a semicolon to delineate names and titles in a complicated sentence.

  The committee included Kevin Tuerff, manager of KTSB Radio; Sharon Justice, dean of students; Laura Sanderson, board member; and Frank Cooksey, mayor.

- Place the semicolon outside quotation marks.

  Mrs. Lang was voted "Coach of the Year"; her students think she should also be "Teacher of the Year."

Question Marks

- Place the question mark inside quotation marks only when it is part of the quotation.

  He asked, "What time does the game start?"

  Have you read "To Build a Fire"?

- Do not use a question mark after an indirect question.

  I wonder when our next quiz is.

Exclamation Points

- Use the exclamation point only rarely after exclamatory sentences, interjections, and emphatic statements.

  The Blue Jays won the State Championship!

- Never use more than one exclamation point at a time.

- Place the exclamation point inside quotation marks only when it is part of the quotation.

  He said, "Get out of here!"

  I love to watch "Home Improvement"!

Apostrophes

- Use an apostrophe in contractions to indicate the omission of one or more letters.

  isn't (is not)

  they're (they are)

- Use an apostrophe to indicate the possessive case of nouns.

  The boy's dog followed him to school.

  The students' radios were confiscated.

- Do not use an apostrophe with possessive pronouns.

  its ("belonging to it"; not "it is")

  hers

  his

  ours

  theirs

  yours

- Use an apostrophe plus *s* to form the plural of letters.

  He got straight A's in Spanish.

- Do not use an apostrophe to form the plural of years and other numbers.

  Test scores have improved since the 1980s.

Dashes

- Use the dash sparingly in news copy.
- Use a dash to indicate a break in thought or the addition of information within or at the end of a sentence.

  Coach Ed O'Hare—a champion debater in his own right—has led the forensic team to victory after victory.

Hyphens

- Use a hyphen to avoid ambiguity.

  I saw a man-eating shark. (a shark that may injure people)

  I saw a man eating shark. (a man having shark for dinner)

- Hyphenate compound adjectives preceding a noun.

  She is a well-known playwright.

- Hyphenate compound numbers and fractions.

  He will be thirty-nine years old.

  Three-fourths of the PTA members are opposed to the resolution.

Quotation Marks

- Use quotation marks before and after direct quotes.

  "I'm not sure what I'll do after graduation," Senior Marina Verdi confessed.

- Use quotation marks at the beginning of each paragraph of quoted matter and at the end of the last paragraph. Do not use quotation marks at the end of a paragraph when the same speaker is quoted at the beginning of the next paragraph.

- Use quotation marks for names of musical compositions, radio and television shows, poems, magazine articles, short stories, and chapters in a book. Use italics for names of books, plays, movies, and magazines. (If italics are not available, quotation marks can be used.)

- Use single quotes for a quotation within a quotation.

  The teacher asked, "Have you read Poe's 'Tell-tale Heart'?"

- Do not use quotation marks for indirect quotations.

  He said he would be a candidate for student council.

- Do not use quotation marks in question-and-answer copy blocks.

  Q: Why did you decide to become yearbook adviser?

  A: I love working with journalism students and teaching them proper style.

Spelling and Usage

- *they're* is the contraction of "they are"
- *their* is a possessive pronoun (*their* books)
- *there* is an adverb of direction or location (over *there*)
- *complementary* means "similar"
- *complimentary* means "free"
- *fewer* refers to individual items (There are *fewer* than 25 $1 bills here.)
- *less* refers to quantity (I have *less* than $25 here.)
- *a lot* is two words (I have *a lot* of homework.)
- *all right* is two words (It's *all right* to express your opinion in the editorial page.)
- Trademarked brand names, such as Coke, Xerox, and Kleenex, should be capitalized and used only to refer to specific brands. Try to use generic equivalents when possible (soft drink, photocopier, tissue).
- An event is not "annual" until it has been offered more than once. There can be no "first annual" event.
- There is only one winner of an award. All others place (She placed third in the swim meet).

Editorial Policy and Guidelines

The school press is governed by the same basic legal rights and responsibilities as the professional press. High-school journalists have the right guaranteed in the First Amendment to free expression, insofar as published items may not contain libel or obscenity, invade the privacy of individuals, or incite or violate the laws of copyright.

With the right to freedom of expression comes an obligation to the highest ideals of the journalistic profession. These include responsibility, freedom of the press, independence, sincerity, truthfulness, accuracy, impartiality, fair play, and decency. Good taste should be exercised in all content.

Stated generally, the goals of student publications at Shawnee Mission North High School are to inform, entertain, interpret (through editorial commentary and bylined articles), and provide a sounding board for ideas and opinions of students and faculty SMN. In addition, it is understood that publications are primarily designed to serve as a laboratory experience for students interested in learning the techniques of sound journalistic practice. While staff members are expected to strive for professional quality, we recognize that they are engaged in an educational venture, and as such, room for trial and error must be allowed.

While the adviser may provide suggestions about content, the final responsibility rests with the editorial board of each publication. This editorial board shall consist of the editors of each publication, with the Editor-in-Chief serving as chairman. Editorial board decisions should use these guidelines as models.

Content Guidelines

1. Publication shall be free of profanity, vulgarity, and words which have acquired undesirable meanings, as judged by the generally accepted standards of the community.

2. Publications shall contain no statements derisive of any race, religion, or national origin.

3. Publications shall show no disrespect for law enforcement nor the generally accepted ethics of the community.

4. Publications shall not advocate illegal acts of any kind.

5. Publications shall avoid editorial material which encourages cheating.

6. Publications shall avoid naming and publicizing students who have violated public law.

7. Expressions of opinion in an article on controversial subjects must be clearly identified as such by means of direct or indirect quotes or by means of a byline. Except for standing columns or occasional news analyses, articles of this nature should be reserved for the editorial page, or other pages clearly labeled as opinion.

8. Unsigned editorials are to appear only on the designated editorial page and are to represent a majority opinion of the editorial board. When an

editorial represents the opinion of the writer only, it shall be signed. All editorials are to conform to acceptable standards of journalistic accuracy and integrity.

9. Letters to the editor are to be signed when submitted to the editorial board. Names may be withheld from publication only with the approval of the editorial board who shall consider the following criteria when making their determination:

   a. The truth of statements made in the letter must be researched by the editors.

   b. Publication of the letter may result in repercussions of a serious nature for the author.

   c. It is generally understood that a letter carrying no signature carries less credibility than one which is signed.

   The paper reserves the right to edit letters for length and repetition. Publication of letters is subject to the laws of libel and defamation, obscenity, encitement, and copyright. Publication of letters will be determined by a majority vote of the editorial board. All letters will be kept on file for one year.

10. To maintain independence and integrity, the publications shall not become involved in, or take sides with, any rivalries or jealousies within the school. No person or organization is to be permitted to use the publications to his or her own ends—be that the editor, a staff member, the adviser, a teacher, the administration, or someone outside the school.

11. If a student's name or picture is used as an endorsement in an advertisement, a release form must be signed by both the student and his or her parents before publication of the endorsement.

12. Paid political advertisements will be accepted with the name of the payee clearly indicated in the advertisement.

13. Advertisements of alcohol and tobacco will not be accepted.

14. Items of a controversial nature will be discussed by the editorial board. Students are expected to take an active interest in the events around them and, accordingly, there are no such things as "taboo" topics. If the editorial board is unable to reach agreement, either an editor or the adviser may refer the subject to the publications board for review, and that group may render a decision about the article's suitability for publication, based upon a strict adherence to guidelines set forth herein.

15. An error of fact in any edition will require a statement of correction in the following edition if deemed appropriate or feasible according to space limitation.

— Shawnee Mission North High School (Mission, Kansas)

Staff Structures and Responsibilities

Newspaper Staff Structure

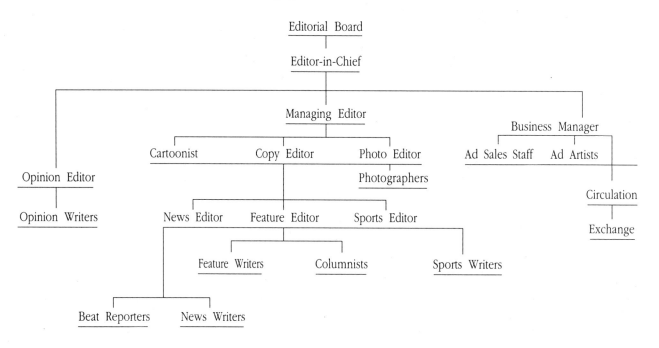

Newspaper Staff Structure

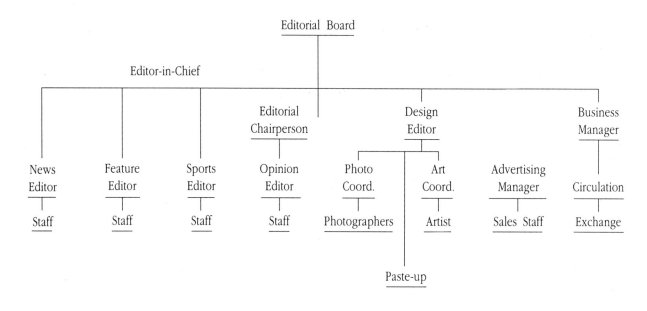

—Grosse Pointe South High School (Michigan)

Staff Organization

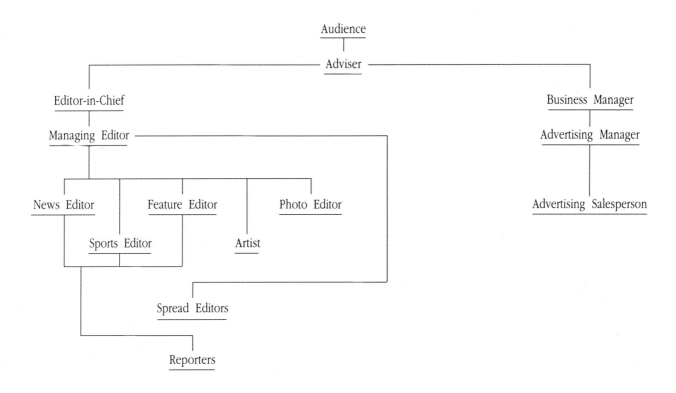

—Lake Highlands High School (Texas)

Staff Responsibilities

Editor-In-Chief
1. General overseer of the entire work of the editorial department.
2. Sees that all news is well balanced, and that some phases of school activities are not receiving too much publicity.
3. Studies each issue of the paper to suggest improvements.
4. Determines the general content of the paper.
5. Logs in story drafts as they come in.
6. With managing editor, plans the headline schedule for the paper.
7. Coordinates the efforts of the head photographer with all other editors.
8. Assigns artwork and assists spread editors in the areas of graphics and design.
9. Keeps a record of all art and photos published.
10. Prepares the nameplate and all folios for pasteup or printout.
11. In consultation with the adviser, fixes policies and rules for the makeup of the paper.

12. Takes charge of the editorial page and column writers.

13. Calls and acts as chairperson of staff and editorial board meetings.

14. Serves as "contact" with the paper's audience, receiving complaints and trying to solve them in the best way possible.

15. Attends school board meetings and/or sends a representative of the paper to school board meetings.

Managing Editor

1. Supervises news, feature, and sports editors.

2. Prepares assignment sheet for reporters.

3. Directs the work of the copyreaders.

4. Directly responsible for Page 1.

Feature Editor

1. Oversees writing of feature articles and in-depth reports, as well as the entertainment section.

2. Plans and oversees distribution of the paper.

3. Organizes and maintains the exchange file.

4. Copyreads all feature material.

News Editor

1. Oversees writing of news articles.

2. Copyreads and edits all news articles.

3. Works with the editor-in-chief on the paper's public relations (birthdays, social events).

Sports Editor

1. Prepares assignment sheet for members of the sports staff.

2. Writes a sports column for each issue of the paper.

3. Becomes personally acquainted with coaches and players in all sports so as to be better qualified to write and assign stories about them.

4. Responsible for knowing rules and terminology of athletic contests in order to interpret them for the writers and audience.

All Editors

1. Offer assistance and guidance to all staff members.

2. Train new staff members.

3. Revise and edit copy prepared for publication.

4. Be willing to write as many stories on any topic that is necessary for the production of the paper.

5. Sell a specified number of column inches of advertising space for each issue of the paper.

Business Manager

1. Sells a specified number of column inches of advertising space for each issue of the paper.

2. Determines the number of pages to be run in each issue according to the total number of column inches of advertising space sold for each issue of the paper.

<table>
<tr><td></td><td>3.</td><td>Keeps account of advertising space sold and contracted for and the collection of such ads.</td></tr>
<tr><td></td><td>4.</td><td>Sends bills to advertisers at least once a month.</td></tr>
<tr><td></td><td>5.</td><td>Keeps account of money collected for advertising space.</td></tr>
</table>

Advertising Manager

1. Sells a specified number of column inches of advertising space for each issue of the paper.
2. Responsible for designing ad space for each issue of the paper.
3. Responsible for ad pasteup for each issue of the paper.
4. Responsible for keeping an accurate run sheet of advertising to be published in each issue of the paper.
5. Along with the Business Manager, is responsible for keeping an up-to-date file of past advertising copy and contracts.

Advertising Salesperson

1. Sells a specified number of column inches of advertising space for each issue of the paper.
2. Responsible for ad design for space sold.

Photography Editor

1. Works with the editor-in-chief in determining photo needs for each issue of the paper.
2. Gives assignments to photo staff members and makes sure that assignments are carried out.
3. Crops and proportions all photographs to be used.

Spread Editor

1. Responsible for the pasteup or printout of assigned pages which includes:
   a. Positioning folio lines and copy on computer or pasteup sheet
   b. Typing in and positioning bylines, photo captions, and photo credits
   c. Noting and typing in all corrections
2. Writes headlines for spread.
3. Proofreads pages for corrections.
4. Plans layout for assigned pages.
5. Works with photographer and artist on photo and art needs for spread.

Artists

1. Prepare artwork for various pages as assigned by editor-in-chief.
2. Prepare editorial cartoon for each issue of the paper.

Reporters

1. Write clear, concise, and accurate reports for all assignments.
2. Turn in two rough drafts and a final copy of stories.
3. Maintain good, open relationships with news sources.

Photographers
1. Take, develop, and print all assigned photos.
2. Maintain an open line of communication with the photo editor, editor-in-chief, adviser, and staff members regarding photographic needs of the paper.

—Lake Highlands High School (Richardson, Texas)

20-Day Production Plan

Monday	Tuesday	Wednesday	Thursday	Friday
1. Ad sales 2. Pages assigned 3. All stories, editorials, features, assigned	1. Ad sales 2. Keyboard folio, masthead information into computer	1. Ad sales 2. Keyboard in calendar of events	1. Ad sales 2. Editorials due 3. Editorial editing 4. Editorial rewrites assigned	1. Ad sales 2. Features due 3. Features editing 4. Feature rewrites assigned 5. Editorial rewrites due 6. Editorials keyboarded

Monday	Tuesday	Wednesday	Thursday	Friday
1. Ad sales 2. Feature rewriting 3. Features keyboarded	1. Ad sales 2. Feature rewrites due 3. Features keyboarded	1. Ad sales 2. News assigned 3. Features keyboarded 4. Late feature rewrites due	1. Ad sales 2. Ads composed 3. Features keyboarded	1. All ads due 2. Ads composed

Monday	Tuesday	Wednesday	Thursday	Friday
1. Print out folios, masthead, standing items 2. News due 3. News edited 4. News rewrites assigned	1. Cartoons, art due 2. News rewrites due 3. Keyboard news 4. Write heads	1. Ad dummies to editor 2. Photos due 3. Keyboard news 4. Late news, rewrites due 5. Keyboard heads 6. Write, keyboard captions	1. Keyboard news 2. Keyboard heads, captions	1. Print out ads 2. Begin page printouts and pasteup

Monday	Tuesday	Wednesday	Thursday	Friday
1. Page printouts 2. Late news due 3. Late news edited, keyboarded 4. Late photos due 5. Heads, captions written, keyboarded 6. All printed pages proofed 7. All corrections keyboarded	1. Print out	1. Final printouts 2. Take paper to printer	1. Begin planning next paper 2. Pick up paper from printer	1. Distribute papers 2. Address, mail exchange papers 3. Bill advertisers 4. Critique paper

—**Courtesy of Taylor High School (Katy, Texas)**

Code of Ethics

SOCIETY of Professional Journalists believes the duty of journalists is to serve the truth.

WE BELIEVE the agencies of mass communication are carriers of public discussion and information, acting on their Constitutional mandate and freedom to learn and report the facts.

WE BELIEVE in public enlightenment as the forerunner of justice, and in our Constitutional role to seek the truth as part of the public's right to know the truth.

WE BELIEVE those responsibilities carry obligations that require journalists to perform with intelligence, objectivity, accuracy, and fairness.

To these ends, we declare acceptance of the standards of practice here set forth:

I. Responsibility:

The public's right to know of events of public importance and interest is the overriding mission of the mass media. The purpose of distributing news and enlightening opinion is to serve the general welfare. Journalists who use their professional status as representatives of the public for selfish or other unworthy motives violate a high trust.

II. Freedom of the Press:

Freedom of the press is to be guarded as an inalienable right of people in a free society. It carries with it the freedom and the responsibility to discuss, question, and challenge actions and utterances of our government and of our public and private institutions. Journalists uphold the right to speak unpopular opinions and the privilege to agree with the majority.

III. Ethics:

Journalists must be free of obligation to any interest other than the public's right to know the truth.

1. Gifts, favors, free travel, special treatment, or privileges can compromise the integrity of journalists and their employers. Nothing of value should be accepted.

2. Secondary employment, political involvement, holding public office, and service in community organizations should be avoided if it compromises the integrity of journalists and their employers. Journalists and their employers should conduct their personal lives in a manner which protects them from conflict of interest, real or apparent. Their responsibilities to the public are paramount. That is the nature of their profession.

3. So-called news communications from private sources should not be published or broadcast without substantiation of their claims to news value.

4. Journalists will seek news that serves the public interest, despite the obstacles. They will make constant efforts to assure that the public's business is conducted in public and that public records are open to public inspection.

5. Journalists acknowledge the newsman's ethic of protecting confidential sources of information.

6. Plagiarism is dishonest and unacceptable.

IV. Accuracy and Objectivity:

Good faith with the public is the foundation of all worthy journalism.

1. Truth is our ultimate goal.

2. Objectivity in reporting the news is another goal, which serves as the mark of an experienced professional. It is a standard of performance toward which we strive. We honor those who achieve it.

3. There is no excuse for inaccuracies or lack of thoroughness.

4. Newspaper headlines should be fully warranted by the contents of the articles they accompany. Photographs and telecasts should give an accurate picture of an event and not highlight a minor incident out of context.

5. Sound practice makes clear distinction between news reports and expressions of opinion. News reports should be free of opinion or bias and represent all sides of an issue.

6. Partisanship in editorial comment which knowingly departs from the truth violates the spirit of American journalism.

7. Journalists recognize their responsibility for offering informed analysis, comment, and editorial opinion on public events and issues. They accept the obligation to present such material by individuals whose competence, experience, and judgment qualify them for it.

8. Special articles or presentations devoted to advocacy or the writer's own conclusions and interpretations should be labeled as such.

V. Fair Play:

Journalists at all times will show respect for the dignity, privacy, rights, and well-being of people encountered in the course of gathering and presenting the news.

1. The news media should not communicate unofficial charges affecting reputation or moral character without giving the accused a chance to reply.

2. The news media must guard against invading a person's right to privacy.

3. The media should not pander to morbid curiosity about details of vice and crime.

4. It is the duty of news media to make prompt and complete correction of their errors.

5. Journalists should be accountable to the public for their reports and the public should be encouraged to voice its grievances against the media. Open dialogue with our readers, viewers, and listeners should be fostered.

VI. Mutual Trust:

Adherence to this code is intended to preserve and strengthen the bond of mutual trust and respect between American journalists and the American people.

The Society shall—by programs of education and other means—encourage individual journalists to adhere to these tenets, and shall encourage journalistic publications and broadcasters to recognize their responsibility to frame codes of ethics in concert with their employees to serve as guidelines in furthering these goals.

CODE OF ETHICS
(Adopted 1926; revised 1973, 1984, 1987)

Index